# THE
# CRISIS
# TURNA
# ROUND

Lead through crisis and position
your company for strength.

## JEFF HILIMIRE

First printing 2020

*Book design by Michael Stanley and Najdan Mancic*

ISBN 978-1-7338689-4-5

Published by Ripples of Hope Publishing
www.ripples.media

"I think you have one time around, and I don't know what's going to be in existence in six months or a year, so I think that you're here on Earth to make some kind of contribution ... I'm impatient, I suppose I wish everybody would be impatient."

—*Bobby Kennedy*

# DEDICATION

*For Ryan, who I never thought I'd be leading through a crisis without...*

# CONTENTS

**FOREWORD** ............................................... **9**

**PRELUDE** ................................................ **11**

**SECTION ONE: BEGIN THE BEGIN** ............. **13**

Find the Right Words .................................... 14

The Preparation ......................................... 15

The Speech .............................................. 21

The Mindset ............................................. 25

Working from Home ...................................... 29

Financial Planning ...................................... 33

**SECTION TWO: GET OUT THE MAP** ............. **43**

Open-Book Management .................................. 44

Windmills vs. Walls ..................................... 47

Weekly Huddle .......................................... 50

Bank Relationship ....................................... 58

Keep Learning .......................................... 60

Doing Good ............................................. 63

Day Hacking ............................................ 65

Seek Advice from Mentors ............................... 68

Focus .................................................. 72

Taking the First Big Hit ................................. 75

Delivering Bad News .................................... 78

Community Service Day .................................. 81

Relieving Stress .................................................. 86

Learning to Pivot ............................................... 91

The Power of Networking ................................. 94

A Devastating Blow ......................................... 96

The Big Moment ............................................... 99

## SECTION THREE: SCARRED, BUT SMARTER .... 102

Back to Normal-ish .......................................... 103

Lessons Learned ............................................. 106

Cash is King ................................................... 108

## EPILOGUE ............................................. 110

## THE 5-DAY TURNAROUND PRELUDE .......... 114

## APPENDIX .............................................. 124

## ACKNOWLEDGMENTS ............................. 134

## ABOUT THE AUTHOR ............................. 136

# FOREWORD

## BY HALA MODDELMOG

*Former President and CEO of Susan G. Komen® & the Metro Atlanta Chamber*

L ike any business leader, I have dealt with my fair share of crises throughout my career. I remember exactly where I was when I first heard about the 9/11 attacks and felt the same heaviness realizing the scope of the coronavirus pandemic. In both situations and so many others, I knew that my next steps as a leader were crucial. Because when uncertainty strikes our world, most of us look to our leaders—whether business, political, community, or spiritual—to help us uncover the *why* of our circumstances and to navigate our efforts to rebound.

Today, that role for leaders has gotten even more complex. The very nature of how we identify and describe a crisis has evolved. With the predominance of social media and the 24/7 news cycle, what once might have been quickly contained or handled internally can become a global concern in a matter of seconds. Everyday citizens are more outspoken about issues they feel passionately about and use every platform available to rally support or influence changemakers.

People, including employees, are also keener to hold their leaders accountable, especially during a crisis. I follow workforce trends, including how the next generation views their employers. Many millennial and Gen Z workers won't even consider working for a company they feel lacks a social responsibility focus or is not in some way striving to impact the world beyond their bottom line.

The lesson here is that we cannot check our humanity at the door, no matter how dire or all-consuming the circumstances may be. And while we're working to get to the other side of the crisis, we should be process-focused, not only outcome-focused, all while staying poised under pressure. I know that sounds like a tall order. So, how exactly is all that done?

Enter *The Crisis Turnaround*. Drawing on his experience leading a company focused on innovation as well as on creating resources and opportunities for businesses to do good in their communities, Jeff has taken some time-honored truths and given us a fresh way of interpreting how we can use them for positive impact in today's volatile environment. Captured with creativity and brimming with authenticity, this thoughtful narrative delivers lessons that any leader can relate to and learn from in their day-to-day work to lead high-performing teams when—not if—a crisis strikes.

# PRELUDE

**W**e first meet our protagonist, Will, in *The 5-Day Turnaround*. He's the CEO of a six-year-old digital ad agency. Through the course of the story, Will guides his friend Matt to think and lead like an entrepreneur. Matt is the chief marketing officer at a large corporation, so the assignment is taxing. To make matters more challenging, it's an assignment that Will navigates while also managing his own company.

This book is set a year before the story of Will and Matt in *The 5-Day Turnaround*. Will is dealing with an uncharted, unimaginably difficult situation. And it's one that is reshaping the entire world. Will, like many others, is looking at an impending global recession, the likes of which has never been experienced. A pandemic threatens to kill hundreds of thousands, shuts down entire countries, and forces people to quarantine at home for months. It's created massive unemployment, driven consumer confidence to new lows, and slowed projects and client spending dramatically. The situation is causing titanic economic ramifications, especially for young, small businesses.

Will is only five years into running his business and (like most) has no idea how to lead his company through this singular time. He is being tested more than ever before. Relying on advice from friends, the culture he has put in place, his instincts, and good old-fashioned fail-and-learn-while-doing, Will does his best to navigate through this crisis.

Perhaps his story is one that will resonate. Let's get into it.

# SECTION ONE:
# BEGIN THE BEGIN

# Find the Right Words

**"It is important for you all to know that we have been building our company for this exact moment, even if we weren't aware of it before."**

I paused and looked at my leadership team. It seemed like a lifetime ago that I had planted my flag in the digital ad agency industry, starting with nothing more than a dream to control my destiny and a few credit cards that offered a tiny, but significant, financial runway. Granted, five years is a long time for a company to stay in business—most small businesses never make it past year one. As I faced this crisis, which was unexpected in the speed of its arrival and the size of its impact, five years felt like an eternity. It also felt like it might not be enough of a foundation.

Truth be told, I had rehearsed this speech. It didn't matter. I'd learned in my short time as a CEO that words are essential, but I was still nervous. After all, it might be months before our people would be together in person again. It was the last day before the mandated work-from-home quarantine went into effect, and it was imperative to set the stage for the battle we were about to wage.

I knew that soon, I'd have to give the same motivational speech, but to the whole company. I needed to be ready.

---

**KEY POINT: As a leader, whenever you are talking with your team, prepare. This is especially important during a crisis. Words are important.**

---

# The Preparation

A few days before delivering the speech of my career, I met up with my mentor Charles at our local coffee spot, The Steaming Cup. I needed to prepare for this unprecedented time, and I knew I could trust his experience and counsel.

I shared with him that I needed to be ready to talk with my people and that I wasn't feeling prepared or confident yet. His response confirmed that the situation was as critical as my instincts were telling me. (It wasn't a source of comfort, but honesty was a good place to start.)

Charles shook his head and rubbed his hands on his jeans. "Will, in all my time, I've never seen anything like this." He paused thoughtfully. "What you say to the team will be really important. The key will be to start by showing how you will begin this crisis."

"Begin?" I asked, unable to hide my confusion. "It doesn't feel like we're beginning this. It feels like we've been thrust into it. There was no warning, for us or anyone! And we're the lucky ones. We can work remotely." I looked around at this cafe we loved. "Think about the people running this cafe...they'll have to shut down completely!"

We were silent for a minute as that sunk in. Entire industries would be devastated by this crisis. Every non-essential business had been ordered to close down its physical operation in a week's time. My clients in the travel and restaurant businesses were terrified.

"Of course, there is a beginning," he said. "You and your company will have to start to deal with this crisis. There will be a middle, and there will be an end. Just like anything, I suppose." Charles studied my response.

"And how exactly am I supposed to think about the beginning of this?" I asked. I am sure the stress and anxiety I was feeling were keeping me from fully realizing what Charles was trying to get me to understand.

"You need to show the team exactly how your company will lean into this phase. Share the things about the business that will allow you to have a strong start. Help them to picture the end. Actually, that's probably the simple part. It's the middle you really need to face. You won't be able to tell them how you'll get through the changes."

He said all this without the faintest hint of sarcasm, which I found a bit unnerving. What the heck was he talking about?

"Okay, Charles. Before we tackle the 'middle,' as you call it, can we go back to the start?" I was anxious and motivated to do this right. I was picking up steam. "How does one start to face an unpredictable, unprecedented crisis?"

"How do you start to tackle any big problem you face as a company?" he asked.

"I guess we lay out the challenge and then begin to problem-solve," I said.

He gave me a small frown, reminding me of the way my third-grade teacher used to look at me when I made a wisecrack in class. "Before that," he said.

I took a deep breath, exhaled, and thought about it. And then it hit me. "We start with our purpose."

He smiled at me. "Which is?"

"To inspire happiness. We always go back and remind ourselves to remember our purpose of inspiring happiness when we're digging deep on a problem," I said.

I was getting it. Our agency had a fully-developed **Purpose, Vision, Tenets, and Values (PVTV)** system.[1] It was a model that Charles had taught me years back. He had invented this framework and used it to successfully shape all of the companies he'd founded and grown.

"So that's your start." He sat back and asked two challenging questions, "How would a company whose purpose is to inspire happiness begin an unprecedented crisis? How would that company create a plan for survival when there is no real way to know how long the crisis will last nor how deep it will go?"

I took a second to think instead of giving into my gut reaction, which was to throw up my hands and say, "*Who the hell knows, Charles? If you're so smart, why don't you tell me?*" I closed my eyes and took another deep breath. "We'd start by thinking about the things that would inspire our team's happiness. That's how we always approach things. Is this going to inspire happiness in our team members? How can this make our team happier?"

"Right," said Charles. "And how would you think about that in this situation?"

"I'd want to be as honest and open as possible with them. That's what they'll need. Even if that means admitting I don't know exactly what will happen, I need to be honest with them."

---

[1]  You can learn more about PVTV in the first book in The Turnaround Leadership Series, *The 5-Day Turnaround*. Find it at www.5dayturnaround.com.

He smiled. "Bingo. Dig deep into how your team has prepared for this particular problem. Believe it or not, you have a lot of things in place already that will help you start strong. Explain your plan and how you and the leadership team are getting prepared. Remind them of your PVTV and how it's going to help," he said.

---

**KEY POINT: At every major decision point, go back to your company's or team's purpose. Having a credible, honest purpose is the key to building a great team, and it is required to survive in a real crisis.**

---

I was nodding and writing in the notebook I always brought to my meetings with Charles. The value of the wisdom he had shared with me over the many years as my mentor was immeasurable. Now was no exception.

I continued, "Okay, that gets us started. I have no idea what we'll look like after this is over. How can I show them a vision for how we'll come out of this?"

"Let's start with what you *can't* predict," he said.

"For one, I don't know how long it will last. I don't know if we'll be able to retain our entire staff, or if they'll have to take pay cuts. I have no idea if we'll be in debt because we made some bad bets, and I can't be sure we'll be able to keep our office space." I put my head in my hands. "I feel like I don't know *anything* about how this will end," I said, probably a little more dramatically than I intended.

Charles sipped his coffee, nodded his head, and said, "That's true. You don't. Nobody does. Put that aside. Think about what you *can* say will happen at the end of this."

I paused and then shrugged. "I honestly don't know."

"Sure, you do. Let me ask it this way: how will you behave?"

"Behave? The same way, I hope." I wasn't getting his point.

He continued to prod me patiently, "Which is to say..."

"Which is to say, I guess I won't become a heartless leader. I'll still care about my team. I'll still be me."

"Because you have a certain moral character that won't be changed just because things get tough?" he asked rhetorically.

"Right. Exactly."

"And how will your company behave? If only you had already defined standards for your team..." He trailed off, exaggerating a quizzical look, tapping his finger on his mouth as if pondering deeply.

I laughed. "Okay, yes, we have values. Good point."

"Remind me what they are again," he said.

"Our values are *Team First, Think Positively, Celebrate Diversity, Do Good,* and *Have Fun.*"

"Great. Do you think those values will guide your behavior during this period?"

"You bet, especially because now I'll be remembering to reinforce them even more."

"Okay then," he said. "Spend time thinking about how that list will help you paint a picture for your team of what you can promise will happen at the end of this crisis."

"Fair enough," I said. I was skeptical, but Charles had never steered me wrong before. I made some more notes, and then came back to the really hard problem. "So what about the 'middle'?"

"As we said before, the middle is the hard part because you don't know what will happen. Ironically, that not knowing also kind of makes the middle the easy part. You can tell your team how you'll start, and you can tell them how you expect things will end up. What you can't tell them is what it will look like as you're getting from one point to the other. That's because it's up to them. Make that clear. They are the ones who will dictate what the middle looks like."

I was jotting notes as fast as I could. My brain was spinning. What Charles said made sense. We had a purpose, values, and guiding tenets. My team just needed to know that it was their plan for action. I always appreciated the ability to give my team a rallying cry, and this would definitely be one.

We finished our coffees, talked a bit more, and then headed for our cars. (Well, I headed to my car. Charles got on his bike. That guy.)

---

**KEY POINT: Tell your team how you're going to start strong, what you envision the end will look like, and that the middle is up to them. Paint an optimistic picture and remind them of their strong foundation. They need something or someone to give them guidance and confidence, and something to act on.**

---

I had worked hard over the last week to find the right words to say to the team. I thought it might be the most critical speech I ever gave to them because I couldn't imagine that we'd ever face a scarier time than this.

# The Speech

**"It is important for you all to know that we have been building our company for this exact moment, even if we weren't aware of it before."**

I paused and looked around the room at all the faces of our agency's team members.

Just like before, I had rehearsed this speech. And I was just as nervous. We didn't know how long it would be, but we did know the mandated work-from-home quarantine would last a while.

Charles had reminded me that words are important, and talking with the leadership team earlier that day had confirmed it. I'd prepared for this. We had the right words to use as our guide. It was up to me to bring everyone along.

"Let us start by remembering that our purpose is to *inspire happiness through positive relationships, impactful work, and doing good.*"

I paused, and the company joined in. "Our vision is to be *sought after by the world's best companies for our creative problem-solving. We will do this by attracting and retaining exceptional people, building remarkable products and experiences, and striving for operational excellence.* We believe in *putting the team first, thinking positively, celebrating diversity, doing good, and having fun.*"

We always started each meeting by reciting our PVTV. I was proud of this team.

Smiling, I continued. "And we have to keep in mind that we are building a *forever* company. We need to react swiftly and smartly during these times, but also keep the long-term view in mind. It'll be critical as we go through the months of uncertainty ahead of us."

I had their attention, so I kept going.

"You know we've focused hard on having a strong, meaningful purpose, woven deeply into the core of our company. All those fun ways we've brought it to life—the t-shirts, the songs, the challenges—they're all going to help remind us of the importance of our purpose as times get hard over the next days and weeks, and maybe even months. We have to lean into our purpose right now, more than ever."

The faces were looking at me and one another, intently and with a little worry starting to show. I took a deep breath, mentally reminded myself of the power of these words, and continued.

"What does that look like? Well, let's start by inspiring happiness in each other. Your teammates will need you, and you'll need them. And our partners will need our grace, our honesty, and our attention. Remember, they're going through this as well."

"We're prepared for this moment because we're comfortable with seeing and reacting to our financials. When we initially decided to make our financials transparent and to educate everyone on financial literacy, we didn't do it because we knew one day we'd face a massive economic crisis. We did it because it's the right way to run a business. We did it because we want everyone to feel like a trusted, important part of the company. But right now, with what we're all about to go through, it will prove to be one of the smartest things we've done. Because you'll see the real-time financial changes we experience, and you'll be able to help us prepare and problem-solve our way through it."

We had maintained open-book management for years. It wasn't always easy, but it was one of the biggest drivers of our financial success year after year and a reason for our industry-leading employee retention numbers. Every Wednesday morning, we have "The Huddle" when we dig into the numbers and important updates as a company. It has become our town hall, with a financial bent.

"Without a doubt, our focus on 'striving for operational excellence' has put us in a strong cash position and has kept our business lean and mean. Our weekly Huddles will be even more vital for digging deep into the numbers. And I encourage you, as always, to ask the tough questions when we meet."

I knew we had the tools we needed to start strong. And I believed we were as prepared as we could be.

"It's not enough to start strong, gang. We also have to try to visualize the ending as clearly as we can. Honestly? I don't know how this will end. But I can tell you one thing for sure. Our number one priority will be taking care of each other. And I guarantee that we'll be even more open with our numbers and decisions than ever before."

"We will be a stronger team in the end. We will have gone through a very trying and stressful time, and we will have done it together. We will do it with grace. I believe we will be better stewards of our business in the future thanks to the new strategies and process improvements we come up with during this period. And I believe our relationships will be stronger than ever because our partners will have seen us help them in whatever way we can."

I'd painted a good picture. People were nodding. But it was time for the tough part—the middle.

"Here's what I don't know...actually, what none of us knows. We can't predict the middle. We're going to start strong, and we will come out with our heads held high. We will be stronger and better for it. But the time in between is the hard work, and that will be up to all of us. We'll stay true to our purpose and continue to deepen our belief in why we're all a part of this company. We will remain diligent about adhering to our values. And we will continue to make smart, sound decisions with the end in sight. And if we do, we will make it through this."

I took a deep breath and nodded. There were some teary eyes. My leadership team was holding steady. We were facing this together.

"I love you all. I am here for you. And I know we will be there for each other every step of the way. Now, let's do this."

And then we packed up our things and left the office unsure of when we'd see each other again. Even unsure who among us would actually be coming back.

I was the last one to leave, and while I locked up, I took one final look around.

Let's do this, indeed.

# The Mindset

If I was going to lead this company through a crisis, I needed to make sure I had the right mindset.

During a crisis, a leader has several functions. The most important one is to protect the health of the company and the wellbeing of every team member. That takes balancing the long-term implications with the short-term decisions we need to make to survive.

I would need to stay on top of the finances and the revenue projections, keep an eye on the expenses to make sure we're frugal, and monitor cash flow to ensure we can stay alive as a business. And while doing that, I would have to make sure we're not cutting off our nose to spite our face. We would have to be careful not to make short-sighted decisions that could restrict our ability to remain the company we want to be in the long run.

Should be easy enough. *(Even my inner monologue has sarcasm.)*

---

**KEY POINT: Short-term decisions will need to be made during a crisis to stay alive as a business. Always weigh those against the long-term ramifications and never forget who you are. Integrity is key.**

---

I couldn't let myself get lost in the X's and O's. The numbers would be significant, but it would also be critical to help the team have hope along the way. I would have to make sure that we all remained positive and collaborative and to keep from getting overly focused on the numbers. I would have to keep a pulse on how everyone was feeling and how the culture was faring, and share hope.

And I needed to stay very close to my leadership team. This time would be stressful and anxiety-ridden. They all felt so accountable to the rest of the group. I would have to use video conferencing quite a bit to keep some personal connection. They needed to know that I'm here and that I have their back.

---

**KEY POINT: As a leader, especially during a crisis, you need to make sure you're focused on the operational aspects of the business and the emotional state of the team. Stay close to your leadership. They are on the front lines. They're your primary source of insight about the state of the culture. And they'll need you more than ever.**

---

The future was uncertain, and the world was upside down. Now was the time to worry. It wouldn't be easy to balance being honest with the team and maintaining my natural optimism. I was thankful for the fact that I reserved my concern for when it was warranted. It kept me clear-headed and comfortable taking the risks I knew I'd have to.

I was lucky in that I pretty much always see the glass as half full, and it usually has something better in it than water. Obstacles are opportunities. Problems are challenges and chances to grow. Losses make you stronger.

Generally, I've believed that if I take a risk and it doesn't pay off, I'll end up in a better place than I was before. Maybe I'll learn something new. Perhaps I'll be forced to take my life in a new direction that will bring excitement and new opportunities. Maybe what I thought was going to be the best outcome wasn't the best at all. Regardless, I'd have learned and kept moving forward.

Having my own business has helped me be a positive person. I recognized early on that if I was upset about how bad things were—and at times, things got really bad—that everyone in the company would have the right to do the same thing. So I forced myself to look on the bright side. Were we losing a client? Okay. That's tough, but not the end of the road. We would put our focus on our other clients and even knock out those side projects that had been sitting and waiting.

Case in point: At the end of year one of the business, we had signed a contract with a company to do a major website. Our largest project to that point was about $1,500. This project was for $65,000. We thought it was the greatest thing that had ever happened to us. We got office space. We hired someone. We changed everything. Then a month in, that client went bankrupt. We never got a penny. At that moment, it felt like everything was going to fall apart. But I fully believe losing that account was the best thing that ever happened to our company. It forced us to make our business work.

Up to that point, we were working hard, but we hadn't been "all in." I still had a part-time job to pay bills, one of our partners was working remotely, our "office" was in my basement, etc. After that point, we were locked in, and we made it happen. We kicked all sorts of butt, never had a year where we didn't grow, and four years later, here we are. Worst thing ever? Or the best thing ever?

When you are positive, things work out better than if you're not, if for no other reason than your perspective makes it seem better. I honestly think that if you are happy and positive and confident, things tend to work in your favor more often than not. Anyway, it has worked for me so far.

And I was going to need to show my team that even though I might be worried about this crisis and even though the future was uncertain, I was confident and determined. You have to model the behavior you want to see in your team. And we'd all need to keep a positive attitude to make it through.

---

**KEY POINT:** A positive, optimistic leader is magnetic. People want to follow them. This may not be a natural state for you, and it will likely be more difficult during times of high stress, but keep in mind that your team is watching you for signs of how to behave. You can do this.

---

# Working from Home

It only took about a half-hour of working from home that first morning for me to realize I needed a plan. The distractions were everywhere. I slept in longer than usual, then spent time talking with my wife Sarah about the bizarre state of the world.

Sarah would be busier than usual, chasing our three-year-old Danielle around the house. I would have enjoyed joining in on that fun, but I had my own work to do. I had a team and a business to lead through this crisis, and I needed to work. It wasn't going to be business as usual—business was definitely *unusual*. I could barely leave my house, much less head to the office early in the morning.

To get anything done, I'd need some rules.

## Rule #1—Have a place to work in the house.

Having a set place to work would be crucial. Usually, I loved working on the kitchen counter, being in the hustle and bustle of the household. But I also knew that was a very distracting space and wouldn't work for a prolonged period (or video calls). I spent the next fifteen minutes organizing my little-used home office to make it feel more workable. It didn't take long to realize how lucky I was to have a quiet space to work.

## Rule #2—Make the bed and get dressed.

A little bit of research on the topic of working from home helped me see that one of the tricks is to make it seem like you're actually going to work. Making your bed and showering and getting dressed seemed to make people more productive. Since I was determined to be my usual productive self, I got to cleaning myself up.

## Rule #3—Be clear about work time and hang-out time.

I could already see the problem of signaling when daddy was available, and when he wasn't. I decided to give myself some clear boundaries. I would work from 7:30 a.m. until noon, and then I'd take a one-hour lunch break. Then back to work from 1:00 p.m. until 2:30 p.m., when I'd take a half-hour to check in with the family. After that, work from 3:00 p.m. to 6:00 p.m.

At that point, my goal would be to shut "work" down for the night. Maybe I'd check in around 9:00 p.m. to see if there was anything my team needed from me. Previously when I worked from home, I was very inconsistent with my availability for work and my family. I was determined to draw that line more clearly this time around.

## Rule #4—Embrace the flow to be more productive.

I know me, and I know that there are times when I am super productive and times when I struggle with distractions and, well, laziness.

Years ago, I wrote a huge article and speaking series about leadership. As I was working on the plan for it, I was worried that I'd fall prey to distractions. Writing can be a lonely process, and because you don't *have* to write it, it's easy to find other things to do.

An article I read about building habits suggested committing to writing every day. So I made the plan: I would sit down every single morning and write for at least fifteen minutes. If I didn't feel it at the end of fifteen minutes, I would stop. If I had a good groove going, I'd keep at it.

Sure enough, the first few mornings, I just kinda felt bored writing and stopped after the set amount of time. But on the third morning, I didn't even look up to check the time. Well more than an hour had passed. I kept writing and didn't stop for two hours. The time flew.

I kept with that routine for weeks. Some mornings it was fifteen minutes, and I was just done. The words wouldn't come, and I found myself thinking of other things. And then other days I would write for over three hours, only stopping because I was ready for lunch.

By the end of thirty days, I had my first draft complete. And that was when I realized that by embracing the flow, I could relieve myself of the "distraction guilt" and lean into those times when I was really feeling it.

That experience taught me it's ok not to "feel it" every day. Sure, there are days when you just have to accomplish a task or goal. On those days, find an accountability partner or post it publicly to give yourself more pressure.

But other times, it's acceptable to have an off day or two. The trick is, when you're in the zone, move everything else out of the way and allow yourself to go deep. Maybe give yourself two hours on the calendar for the work, and if you just can't push past fifteen minutes, give yourself the rest of that time to accomplish other things.

That was how I was going to approach working from home. I would lean into the times I was in the zone, and I'd be comfortable switching to a new task if I didn't feel it.

## Rule #5—Lots (and lots) of video calls.

I've never been a big video conference person. I think it was always easier to make a phone call, but that was when I could also see people face-to-face periodically. And there were always good excuses in the past to avoid them (like the Wi-Fi bandwidth was too slow or the video software was buggy). At this point, there were no good reasons not to use video calls, so I decided to require everyone on my team—myself included, to use video calls so we could be 'together.'

---

**KEY POINT: When working from home, be purposeful about productivity. Find ways that work for you, even if it requires 'tricking' yourself into it.**

---

# Financial Planning

Early in the crisis, I met with my head of operations and finance, Rachel, to map out a financial game plan. It was not a meeting we wanted to have, but we knew that detailing a disaster scenario could end up being a key to survival. The difficult situation wouldn't avoid us if we buried our heads. The reality was that many companies would have to slim their ranks. While it seemed unthinkable, we had to be realistic about the idea that we might have to let go of some of our team members too. We loved them all, and the idea of any one of them being unemployed during an economic crisis was a tough pill to swallow.

---

**KEY POINT: Create a financial and operational plan going into a crisis. Even if you alter it as you go, it is crucial to take the time to consider all the details when you aren't in the throes of a recession—or any disaster, for that matter. Having a plan will give you peace of mind and allow you to make better decisions in the future.**

---

Our first planning session focused on the pipeline. Rachel was, as usual, ready to go and waiting for me.

"Hey, Will. Were you able to get any customer updates from Steve?" she asked.

We had agreed that I would talk to our head of client relationships, Steve. He would offer a read on how our clients might be adjusting their budgets and planning based on the mandated work-from-home situation and economic uncertainties that were beginning to bubble up.

I nodded. "Yep. And I also caught up with Ahmet to hear how the sales pipeline looked." Ahmet was our head of business development.

"Great. How's it looking?"

"Steve pointed out that one of our strengths heading into this is that we have a very diverse client set." We had focused hard on that from a revenue perspective, never wanting any client to be more than about a sixth of our business in case the relationship ended. But we had also made diversity a priority in terms of the industries we support. "We're lucky on that level," I said.

At that point, we didn't know what would happen, but if history offered any insight, it was that some industries would get hit hard and others would come through okay. Some might even thrive as a source of necessary support. By having companies from all different sectors in our portfolio, we had some confidence that we could keep a balance.

---

**KEY POINT: Make sure you have diversity in your client base. That means controlling the percentage of revenue a client comprises, varied deal structures, and a spread across multiple industries. This diversity will help when trouble hits, crisis or otherwise.**

---

"And Ahmet?"

"Ahmet remains—how did he put it?—'cautiously optimistic.' He said that the pipeline is still strong. We have several proposals with companies that don't think they'll be quite as affected by all of this as others, but he's sure things will start to slow down as companies begin to feel the ramifications of this pandemic."

She nodded and began to write. "Did you ask them both for their guess on Scenario Two?"

We had mapped out three financial scenarios:

Scenario One would be a small five percent drop in revenue.

Scenario Two would be a 'most likely to occur scenario' with a deeper drop.

Scenario Three would be a worst-case scenario.

Rachel and I would work up our best guesses for the second and third scenarios. Steve and Ahmet would give theirs. Then we'd average them out.

"Yes. Steve said he expects between a fifteen and twenty percent drop in revenue from existing clients. Ahmet thought we could see a forty percent drop in new business. I'm guessing more like twenty percent," I said.

Rachel thought for a moment. "Okay, with my twenty-five percent estimate, we're looking at a projected," she paused and checked her math on the calculator, "twenty-six percent drop in revenue. Let's go with twenty-five to keep it clean."

She opened up a spreadsheet and created three columns: *Scenario One, Scenario Two,* and *Scenario Three.* Under *Scenario One,* she typed "5% revenue drop," and under *Scenario Two,* she wrote "25% revenue drop."

She then looked back at me and asked the question I was dreading. "What do we want to put for the *Scenario Three* column?"

I stood up and started pacing, which was my habit when I needed to think deeply or make a hard decision. This would be both.

"I do have a number, but I want to give you my reasoning first because I'm guessing your number will be more drastic than mine," I said.

"That's my job. I have to be the most conservative planner on the leadership team. I don't *want* to be..." She trailed off. It was a recurring theme with Rachel. As the head of finance and operations, being risk-averse was a necessary but tough part of her job—mainly because the rest of us were always more bullish.

"Hey, I know that. We *all* know that! We love you for it, and we *need* that from you. There are plenty of times you helped us from driving right off a cliff. But I do want to explain why my guess on the drop in revenue isn't likely to be as deep as what you'd predict."

"Go for it," she said, eager to change the subject.

"We've stayed focused on new business. Our pipeline remains very strong. I expect leads will slow down, but I don't see them drying up. Businesses still need what we do, and we're good at finding them."

---

**KEY POINT: Focus on growth. Too often, teams will work hard on new business, get some wins, move their attention to other things, only to look up six months later and realize their sales pipeline has dried up. A consistent growth mindset—more than strategy, case studies, or any other sales concept—is the vital area of focus.**

---

"I don't see a massive change in client work across the board. We have worked extremely hard to build trusting relationships with our clients. We'll do right by them during this period. Steve has created an entire playbook about how to be the best partner we can be over the next several months."

Rachel cleared her throat, "Kinda feels like you're stalling here." She winked to show she was mostly kidding.

"Fine. I think we're in as good a spot as we can possibly be. My worst-case scenario is a revenue drop of forty percent."

She smiled at me and said, "That's the same number I came up with."

She put "40%" under the *Scenario Three* column. Last, she wrote the corresponding revenue numbers under each scenario.

"Now we have to decide how profitable or unprofitable we are willing to be during this period," she said. "We have cash in the bank equal to two months of current expenses. And we have the line of credit available with the bank for the same amount."

"Yep. Which goes back to why you're so important to this team," I said, giving a wink back. "I even debated with you last year when you wanted to establish the line of credit. My point was that we didn't need it, and your point was..."

She finished, "that we establish a line of credit or a loan with a bank when you don't need it because they only want to give you credit if you can cover it. The worst time to ask for money from the bank is when you need it."

---

**KEY POINT:** Save at least two months of expenses in cash. Try to establish a line of credit with your bank equal to that amount. You don't have to use it, but you never know when disaster will strike. As your company grows, always look to increase your cash on hand and your line of credit accordingly.

---

"That reminds me," I said. "I've been reading about what will happen in the market and how devastating this might be for all companies, especially banks. It seems like we need to go back to the mantra we kept saying in the early days of our business: cash is king."

"I totally agree," she said. "I have a list of things to try to help us preserve cash. I've set up a time to talk with our landlord to see if we can get a deferment on payments. I've heard that some building owners will let you have a few months of not paying rent in exchange for an extension on the lease. I'll try that."

"I'm also taking the marketing budget down to the bare minimum, and I recommend that we pause our 401k contributions for the foreseeable future. I imagine most team members will be pausing their personal contributions as well," she said.

I hated to pause things like that, but it was the right thing to do. "Yes, let's bounce that off the leadership team. It seems like that's the right approach."

"I'm also going to speak with the bank to see if we can increase our line of credit, just in case. I've been reading that banks may end up restricting loans and lines of credit if things go the way many economists think they will."

"You mean pulling some of the line even if we don't need it? I don't know about that," I said.

"Here's the thing. If we need it, of course, we'll be happy that we have it. And if we don't end up needing it—which will mean things didn't get as bad as we thought—then we won't mind paying a few months of interest on it," she said.

"If we run our business at, let's just say break-even, then we should never need it given the amount of cash we have on hand, right?" I asked.

"Not necessarily," she said. "We might be running at break-even, but if some of our clients aren't able to pay us on time, or at all, then we could have a gap in our cash flow. I think there's a pretty good chance of that happening."

She paused and turned back to her laptop. In just a moment, she'd calculated the amount of interest we'd pay if we pulled half of our line of credit and held it for six months. It wasn't a significant amount, so I agreed. We didn't have any idea what was to come, and giving ourselves the best chance of survival was paramount.

---

**KEY POINT: Do everything you can to preserve cash. Pull from your line of credit, ask your landlord if you can defer rent payments, talk to your vendors, and see if you can get extended payment terms—anything to give yourself more runway to make it through a recession.**

---

We had the line of credit figured out, but we were far from done. "Okay, Will. Now, what about acceptable profitability?" Rachel looked at me quizzically. "What do you think? Should we allow ourselves to break even during this period? Should we try to hold a meager profit, say five percent? Or should we allow ourselves to be slightly unprofitable, dipping into our line of credit or our cash in the bank?"

"I think that we need to allow ourselves to break even for several months before making any changes, using the cash we have to get us through," Will said.

"Okay, Will. Last thing. We have to talk about our largest expense. You know it's our staff."

I had thought about this. I loved our team. The people line item was the most expensive on our P&L. But putting someone out on the street to find a new job in the middle of an economic recession? That would have to be the last resort.

This process was so hard. "Okay, so business survival has to be the priority. If the business goes away, then none of us will have a job. If we're going to take care of our people, we have to take care of the business. We will be careful how we walk that line," I said, partly to make sure we were on the same page, and partly because I was stalling.

Luckily, Rachel jumped in. "What if we come up with an acceptable amount of the cash we can use to keep us at our agreed-on baseline profit margin? And that cash gives us the buffer before we need to do any layoffs?"

"That makes sense," I said. "I feel like the lowest we can go on cash in the bank before we make any cuts would be one and a half months of expenses. That gives us two and a half months of available cash for our buffer. I think we allow ourselves to break even, and we use the available cash to keep us there. The longer we can make the available cash last, the longer before we have to make any layoffs."

"There's a middle option we need to discuss," she said. "We're making the changes we can make now, things like pausing the 401k, reducing marketing spend, and trying to get the rent pushed, but we should also discuss the potential of reducing overall salary as a middle point."

This option was something that I had been thinking about as well. I hated the idea of asking people to take a salary cut, but it was better than laying people off.

"I agree. That's our first step. And I think it is something we do before we start pulling from our cash reserves," I said. I could tell this surprised her.

"Really? I was thinking we pull from our cash reserves and then make the salary cuts, with the last resort being layoffs," she said.

"We could do it that way, but then our runway would be extremely short. Our goal, as I see it, is to give ourselves the best chance to survive this, no matter how long it goes. We need to buy time. If we make twenty percent salary cuts across the board and only pull from our cash reserves if we need to, we'll have a much longer runway."

"Hold up, let me do some math," she said. She hammered on her keyboard for a few minutes. "Okay, if we did a twenty percent salary cut, that two and a half months of cash would actually cover more than three months of expenses."

"Super. If we hit our predicted worst-case scenario revenue drop, how long would that give us before we had to do any layoffs?" I asked.

After another couple of minutes, she said, "That would give us more than six months before we would have to let go of any employees."

"Perfect," I said. "So here is where we are. We will tighten our belts and do what we can to increase our cash position. If we see that we are falling below breakeven, we will implement the twenty percent salary cuts across the board. That gives us two and a half months of cash to keep ourselves at break-even. When that runs out, we will consider layoffs, but only then. How does that sound?"

"It's a solid plan. The hardest part will be to consider what team members we might have to lay off if it comes to that point."

She was right. We spent time talking through that scenario, focusing mostly on how to be as fair as possible with our team members. We started with the science that goes into staffing decisions—like what kinds of work we were doing, which determined the skills we needed to continue earning revenue. But there was a great deal of heart and emotion at play. Our team members were people, not just valuable practitioners.

The reality was, we could try to prepare thoughtfully, but wouldn't really know how this part of the strategy would play out until we were in the middle of it.

We also spent time making plans for how we would support any team members who we did have to lay off. Besides giving them as much severance as possible, we would work hard to help them find a new position. I made a note to get more input on that from our leadership team.

We finished mapping out a complete scenario. It was hard, but we had our plan, and I had to start thinking about how to share it with the team.

---

**KEY POINT: Be willing to think creatively about the things you can do to help keep your company alive. Ideas such as cutting everyone's salary might seem untenable at first, but it might be the best decision if the alternative is laying off team members. Only you will know the right course to take, but make sure you're thinking creatively and evaluating all possible options.**

---

# SECTION TWO: GET OUT THE MAP

# Open-Book Management

I t was the first Monday of the quarantine. Our leadership team meeting was about to kick off, and I was looking forward to 'seeing' everyone on screen.

As a standard practice, we held our leadership team meetings every Monday morning. The all-company weekly Huddle was on Wednesday morning every week. We decided to keep both of those in place as we entered our new work-from-home lives via video conference.

"Good morning, everyone," I said at 9:00 a.m. As usual, everyone was on time because we made latecomers sing or do something else silly.

"Let's kick off with our PVTV. Who wants to do it today?" I asked.

Steve jumped in and nailed it, word for word, resulting in applause around the screen from everyone.

"Thanks, Steve," I said. "And I know I sound like a broken record, but now more than ever, we need to keep our purpose in mind. We need to always be asking ourselves how we can inspire more happiness in each other, our team, our partners, our community, and most importantly, in ourselves."

"Rachel, why don't you kick us off by walking everyone through the dashboard," I said.

We spent about fifteen minutes talking about current clients, how projects were progressing, and how our new business pipeline was looking. After that, Rachel and I went through the three scenarios we had created. Everyone weighed in. It was an expectedly somber discussion, but productive and thoughtful, and ultimately, everyone came to an agreement.

"I know we already share the numbers with people at the weekly Huddle," Ahmet said. "But maybe we should also provide a real-time scoreboard that shows the contingencies we will be sharing with them. We could show all three scenarios so that they could be as informed as possible."

"I'm not sure about that," said Steve. "People might panic if they see the numbers not looking good for the following month. We don't need our team members even more distracted, worrying about the future."

Martha, our head of HR, jumped in. "I think we all have to give the team more credit than that, Steve. They can handle this, and don't you think we want them to be able to make gradual and preparatory changes to their spending and home budgets, just in case?"

The debate carried on for about ten more minutes. I had learned over time to sit back and let my leadership team hash out a problem before I weigh in. Even though I often wish it didn't, my voice as CEO carried more weight, and I didn't want to influence the argument or make it sound like I took a side. In almost every case, the team coalesced around the right idea. This was one such case.

"Okay, that was a great discussion, and it sounds like everyone is on the same page. We will create a real-time dashboard for the entire company to view, and it will have our contingency plans built-in. Let's try to have that ready by Wednesday when we announce the plans in Huddle."

---

**KEY POINT: Consider an open-book management style. It can feel uncomfortable sharing your finances with your team, but it will pay off in spades with increased trust and better problem-solving. Communication builds trust, and trust is what makes any team work.**

---

We were getting close to the end of the meeting. As I always did, I asked, "Does anyone have anything else to share?"

"Yes," said Steve. "Let's stay as close to our clients as possible. I'm talking with Mark on Friday." Mark was the CMO of RedBrick, our largest and longest-standing account.

"Great idea. I'm talking with Shera, too." Shera was the CEO of SalesLive, who we'd been working with for about a year. "Everyone, if you have the chance to check in on a client, please do so. Partnership with our clients and knowledge about how they're doing is everything. If we are blindsided by changes on their end, we limit our ability to make good decisions. The sooner we know, the better we can prepare."

Everyone agreed, and we all disconnected.

---

**KEY POINT: During a crisis, knowledge is everything. Stay close to your customers and partners, and share liberally with your leadership team (and overall team when appropriate). The name of the game is agility. The more you know, the better you can react.**

---

# Windmills vs. Walls

"When the wind changes, some people build walls, and some people build windmills."

My first call after our leadership team meeting was to Charles. We had finished our initial chit-chat, checking in on each other's health and families, and I relayed how the discussion with the team had gone.

That was when he said the thing about the windmills.

"I'm sorry, what? Did you say windmills?" I asked.

"It's a Chinese proverb. I can't remember when I first read it, but it seems especially true right now. It has application to this challenging health and economic climate, but it also resonates with the perspective of living a purposeful, fulfilling life," he said and paused. "So, Will, the question is, are you going to build walls or windmills?"

I wasn't sure. Somehow I was not picking up his gist. But, as usual, he was picking up on mine. So he continued.

"Walls, by their nature, are forced stopping points. We create them to keep something out. They're rigid and, for the most part, unmoving.

"When something difficult happens in your life, when the wind changes, you can decide to build a wall to block the wind. But it only works until the wind changes again. And the wind always changes."

I was getting it. "So, now I have a wall that doesn't do me any good, and I need to build another one."

"Right. So, instead, you could decide to embrace the wind. You could say to yourself, 'I know things are going to change again, and again, and probably again after that…and I better prepare for that change and make it work for me the next time it happens'."

Even though we were talking on the phone, I could picture his face so clearly, looking at me with that fatherly smile and clearly caring about me as if I was his own son.

"That mentality can change everything," he said. "It can help you have more positive relationships with people in your life. It can lead you to business success. It can help you solve short-term problems and long-term ones."

"When the wind picks up, like it is now, with this crisis we are facing, the right answer might be to embrace it, not try to stop it. Find a way to make it work for you. Flip what you perceive to be a problem into an advantage."

I listened as Charles finished his thought.

"That's terrific advice, Charles," I said. "And a perfect analogy. But how will I know if I need a wall or a windmill? Clearly, there are things that we will need to do to weather this particular storm that aren't going to be great long-term solutions."

"Of course. For example, I'm guessing that you're trying to extend payment terms with vendors, maybe even your landlord, right?" He asked.

"That's right; those are the kinds of things that we obviously won't change permanently. They're just there to help us get through this particular time," I said.

"You're probably right, although even in that scenario, perhaps there is a lesson to be learned about always negotiating hard on payment terms in the future because you never know when disaster will strike," he said.

I hadn't thought of that. I made a note to talk to Rachel about that being something we did going forward.

"I get your point, I need to be thinking about how to lean into these new changes, not just put in placeholders as a way to make it through," I said.

We said our good-byes and hung up. Charles always had a way of making me think differently. And I was going to need a healthy dose of thinking differently in short order.

---

**KEY POINT:** Understand when something needs to be changed only for the moment vs. when it can be a change that can help your business overall. Look at big changes, especially during a crisis, as a way to grow and get better. We always learn the most when faced with a challenge.

---

# Weekly Huddle

"Testing, testing, can you guys hear me?" Rachel asked. The leadership team had joined the video conference 15 minutes early to test and make sure everything was ready before our weekly Huddle started.

Looking at the screen, I saw the small group of us in our various settings. Steve was in a golf shirt in what looked like a home office. Ahmet was also in a home office but was wearing a button-down dress shirt. Martha was dressed more casually (like me) in a company t-shirt and was outside on what appeared to be her back porch. Rachel was more formally dressed, and I couldn't tell where she was, only that there was a black wall behind her, making her the most professional looking of all of us.

"Steve, I can't hear you," she said. It appeared that Steve was on mute.

"...oh, how about now, I think I had mute on," Steve said. "Can you hear me now?"

A round of yes's and yep's cascaded through the video chat. We were all learning to work in the best way possible in this new normal.

"Okay, let's make sure this Huddle goes as smoothly as possible," I said. "The main goal is to make sure that the whole team understands the plan we've been working on and that they have the chance to ask questions. We'll start with PVTV, present the typical scoreboard overview, share the plan, and open up for Q&A. Let's end with acknowledgments. That should take up the entire time, but is there anything else that's critical to talk about in this Huddle?"

"As long as we give them time to ask questions, then I think that's it from my side," Martha said.

Everyone seemed to agree, and we went over the specifics of the plan one more time. With five minutes left until Huddle started, we disbanded and zipped off to take care of a few quick things before the meeting got going. I needed a coffee refill, to be sure.

I went into the kitchen, where Sarah was giving Danielle her breakfast. While the current situation we were in with this pandemic was tough from almost all angles, one bright side was that I'd get to see them both much more. I was excited to have lunch with them today—I'd blocked it off on my calendar and everything.

"Almost time for the Huddle?" she asked.

"Yep, just grabbing another cup of coffee," I said.

"It was too bad that you guys had to cancel the big nonprofit day you had set up next month," she said. She was referring to our quarterly 'Do Good' initiative that we had to postpone due to the crisis. We were going to bring together marketing volunteers from the community and help as many nonprofits as we could with their website and digital platforms. Once the work-from-home announcement came, we had to push that off to a later date.

"I know. The team was pretty devastated. There were so many charities that we were going to help," I said.

"What did you decide to do instead?"

"What do you mean? We can't do the event anymore, so we pushed it off," I said.

"Right. But what are you going to do? Your business has always had quarterly efforts to help the community. I assumed you would be doing something to help, especially during this time when there's *so* much need," she said.

I thought about that for a moment. She was right. In all the planning we did, we never considered that we would still do our quarterly community service work.

"And I bet it would make everyone feel good to try to help right now," she continued. "Don't you think?"

"Actually, I do," I said, kicking myself for not thinking of that, and for not asking Sarah for her advice. She'd always helped me navigate tough situations. Having her by my side has made all the difference in my career.

I took a glance at my watch and realized the Huddle was about to start.

"That's great advice. Thanks, honey," I said. I quickly planted a kiss on Danielle's head and rushed back to the meeting.

---

**KEY POINT: During difficult times, rely on those closest to you for support and ideas. You're not alone, and ideas can come from anywhere. Seek input from anyone who will give it to you.**

---

I made it back to my computer just in time for the meeting. I looked at the screen. It was crowded with close to seventy-five faces, all in various locations and setups. It was a joy to see them all.

"Good morning, everyone! Who wants to kick us off with our PVTV?" I asked. I was always hoping a non-leadership team member would step up to the plate.

"I'll do it," said Nicholas, one of our newer team members. He did it, and it was flawless.

"Great job, Nicholas!" I said, truly impressed by not only his ability to memorize our PVTV, but also the boldness to do it in front of the entire company so early in his tenure.

We rolled through the beginning part of the meeting. Rachel took everyone through the current financial numbers, Steve gave an update on client relationships, and Ahmet talked about the sales pipeline. So far, there was only a roughly twenty percent drop in our revenue expectations. I was pretty sure that would continue to decrease, but we could handle a drop that size without having to make any significant changes.

It was my turn to walk everyone through the plan. In these cases, I always thought it was best to be as direct as possible.

"I'm sure you can all see that everyone is trying their best to make sure we are as successful as possible during this crisis. That's great, and we should all be so proud of how we're working together. We also need to make sure we're planning for what happens if revenue drops significantly. The reality is, it could. We're working as hard as possible to keep things stable, but some things will be out of our control during this time, and I want you all to know what our plan is to stay the course," I said.

I then walked them through the three scenarios, explaining that we were essentially in Scenario One, tightening our belt and being as efficient as possible. If our revenue dropped twenty-five percent, we would implement Scenario Two, an indefinite twenty percent salary cut across the board. And if our revenue dropped forty percent, we would have to go to Scenario Three, which was to lay off some of our people.

"I want you all to know, laying anyone off is the last thing in the world that we want to do," I said, trying to make eye contact with as many of our team members as I could. "We're sharing this with you because we value you, and it's important that we are honest with you all. If things get too bad, pay cuts and layoffs are possible. We want you to know how and when that might occur."

I paused again, giving everyone—myself included—a moment to breathe.

"I know this level of honesty about our worst-case scenario planning might cause some anxiety for you, but my hope is that you know you are part of the process and that we will keep giving you the information you need so we all have the best chance for success. More than ever, we'll need everyone coming to the table with ideas."

While I didn't say it, another big reason I wanted to share this with everyone was so they knew we had a plan. Too often, leaders resist sharing their plans because the information is hard to deliver, or they don't trust their team members to respond calmly and thoughtfully. This approach is almost always a mistake.

---

**KEY POINT:** Your team needs to know you have a plan. For the long-term, for the short-term, and certainly during a crisis. Sometimes having a plan is more important than the plan itself.

---

The video screen pinged. Someone wanted to ask a question.

"I see that Kirsty has a question," I said.

"Thanks, Will. I'll admit, this is scary stuff to hear. But honestly, it's not as scary as what I had in my mind, so I guess that's good," she said with a nervous laugh. "My question is, how do you think we should go about problem-solving? I know we will all want to try to see how we can help. Do you have any advice on how we might get started?"

"Great question," I said. "And I know I will sound like a broken record, but I would recommend everyone go back to our PVTV. Honestly, I use it all the time to help me think through challenging situations."

"For instance, think about the tenet that says we will *Strive for Operational Excellence*. We talk all the time about what that means to us. If you go deep into that idea, you'll start to see a lot of ways we can be as prudent as possible and help our profit margin. Or think about our purpose to inspire happiness through positive relationships. Maybe there are ways we can be a better partner to our clients during this challenging time that will help our relationships grow rather than wilt."

---

**KEY POINT:** Always go back to your PVTV: Purpose, Vision, Tenets, and Values (or your specific construct). If you have worked to bring your PVTV to life within your company, it can be the compass that everyone uses to navigate through difficult times.

---

After a few more people asked questions, I turned it over to Rachel.

"Later this week, I will share a live scoreboard that will show you where we are against these three scenarios at any point in time," she said. "We will still have our weekly Huddles, but this will be something that we update in real-time with the trigger points we discussed in today's meeting."

No one had any questions for Rachel, but I could tell from looking at their faces on the screen that they would be eager to see the scoreboard when it was ready. For that matter, so would I.

"Ok, everyone," I said. "Time for acknowledgments."

Years ago, I had introduced the idea of adding acknowledgments to the end of our Huddles. The idea was simple. I opened the floor up for anyone to acknowledge any of their peers. Ideally, they were recognized for our values, but it could be anything.

"I'll go first," I said. I usually didn't go first, but given that this was a video conference instead of an in-person meeting, I thought I should get the ball rolling. "I'll start by acknowledging the leadership team for their partnership and hard work over the last few weeks. I think you all know this, but they carry an immense burden trying to help us steer this ship, and their grace and passion have been nothing short of incredible."

Everyone clapped, and I continued, "And I also want to acknowledge Nicholas for being willing to do the PVTV today! That was both brave and impressive!"

They all clapped for Nicholas, and then Kevin jumped in.

"I want to thank you, Will, and the rest of the leadership team, for being so open and honest with us. As Kirsty said, this is a scary time, but I don't know anyone else who works in a company that is so candid with their team. It really shows you trust us, and that means so much right now."

After that, people went back and forth, recognizing each other for things they had done over the past week. Someone mentioned that a team member realized they were struggling and checked in on them after a tense meeting. Another acknowledged a teammate for over-delivering on an important piece of creative. As usual, I had to cut off the love-fest because we had run out of time.

"Ok, I think our time is up. I appreciate all of you so much, and I want you to know that we're doing everything we can to weather the current climate. We'll absolutely need and welcome your help in identifying solutions along the way. Please, as always, be forthcoming with your ideas," I said.

There was a chorus of good-byes as everyone signed off from the video chat. All things considered, I thought the meeting went well. I was sure that being honest with them was the right move, as it always had been. And ending with acknowledgments, as we had for years, was the right way to end the tough conversation.

---

**KEY POINT:** Find ways for your team members to acknowledge and recognize each other publicly. During a stressful time, this kind of peer support and recognition will go a long way to strengthen bonds.

---

# Bank Relationship

"Great news," said Rachel. "I got Bill on the phone, and he was able to increase our line of credit."

Bill was the manager of the small, regional bank we used.

"Really?" I was shocked, given the uncertain state of the economy. "That's great news!"

"He said that he wasn't doing that for many of his clients, but that we'd been such a great partner over the years that he knew we were good for it," she said.

Even though we had talked about increasing our line of credit as a precaution, I honestly didn't expect it to work.

"You've done such a good job building a close relationship with our bank," I complimented her.

"Well, it's like Charles reminded you. Banks are most likely to be willing to give people money when they don't need it, and building trust with the bank is everything. Since then, I've been connecting regularly with Bill. We talk monthly and get together each quarter for coffee. He's given me great advice along the way, and he trusts me."

"Man, was Charles spot on with that one," I said.

"Sure was. Of course, we don't need the increased line right now, and hopefully, we won't, but I'll sleep a little better at night knowing we have it," she said.

**KEY POINT:** Work to maintain a personal relationship with the account manager at your bank. If that's not possible at your current bank, get a reference and make a change. There will be hard times in your business, and having a personal connection with your banker will be extremely helpful.

# Keep Learning

We were just about done with our leadership meeting. As we were wrapping up, I shared with the team the next book that we would read together. Every quarter, I choose a book based on things that are happening in the business, and things we could learn to grow as leaders and managers. At the end of the quarter, we have an offsite meeting where one of the activities is to review the book and share insights.

I announced the book we would be reading this quarter. It was (appropriately) focused on leading during a crisis.

Steve spoke up. "Uh, seriously? We're not really going to be continuing that right *now*, are we? Isn't there enough going on?" he asked.

I chuckled inwardly. Steve always pushed back at first. He always read the book, but it was usually in an all-night cram session the night before it was due.

"We read these books so that we can be better leaders," I said. "Doesn't it seem like we're being tested more than we ever have? I'd argue that this is the exact time we should be learning how to be better leaders."

"Yeah, but it seems like we should be focusing on things that truly matter right now...like client work," Steve responded.

"I think what Will is saying," Rachel said, "is that how we lead right now, during this crisis, is actually the most important thing we can focus on."

"Right," said Ahmet, jumping in. "I'll admit, the idea of being assigned a book right now seems a bit odd, but I would love to learn how other leaders look at leading during a crisis."

"Okay, okay!" Steve laughed, giving in.

With that decision made, we set a date for a two-hour video version of our offsite. In a month, we'd all have the book read and be ready to discuss it.

As we hung up, I remembered a meeting I'd facilitated with the leadership team of one of the nonprofits I supported in my free time. We were spending a half-day focused on ways to work better together as a team. The meeting was going well. Toward the end of our time, I challenged them. "I assume you'd all agree that the success of your organization is tied directly to how successful you are as leaders? And that the stronger your leadership team is, the more likely you are to hit your goals?"

Head nods from all.

"Great. Other than this meeting, and the one we had earlier in the year, how much time have you spent working on being better individual leaders and on being a stronger leadership team?"

The answer was zero. This team had spent a total of six hours *all year* on being better leaders. And yet, they all agreed that's the most important thing they could be working on.

Unfortunately, in my experience, this is how most companies function. The leaders in the organization work extremely hard, becoming better at running their departments and somewhat better at being managers (through experience). But rarely do leadership teams work on being better leaders.

This oversight is why I spend so much of my time and energy working with my leadership team. I know that the more confident and capable they are, the more they connect with and trust one another, the more they collaborate, and the more they understand what it means to be a leader at our company, the more likely we are to hit our goals.

Learning through reading and discussion is one of the best ways to grow.

---

**KEY POINT:** During a crisis, it's even more important to be growing and learning. Try hard not to stop processes you have in place for this, and perhaps look for new ways to add learning into your time.

---

# Doing Good

We were in month two of the crisis, and there was no end in sight. I was proud of how our team was handling it—staying relatively positive, working hard, and generally being there for one another. But it was still early. I wanted to make sure we were still being true to our purpose of inspiring happiness.

I thought back on that early conversation I'd had with Sarah in the kitchen. She had asked how we would continue to live out our value to 'Do Good' during this time. In all honesty, my first response was to try to shelve the effort. We had our own survival to think about. There would be time to help others once the world was back to normal. Right?

No. Sarah was correct. Besides the growing level of need around us, there also was more to our survival than hitting numbers. Team morale was critical. Seeing our team come together in the face of adversity was one thing, but seeing how energized they got from helping others was a different thing altogether. It was like the entire company had a new pulse of electricity running through it when we were doing good together. We were wired to help.

It started to occur to me that doing good made all the sense in the world. It would help the team's mindset. Many of our team members had extra time as projects were being pushed to later start dates. And many nonprofits were hurting deeply. Doing good seemed especially important now.

I decided then and there that we'd do something. I wasn't sure what, but it seemed like a very *us* thing to do. I would bring it up at our next leadership team meeting and see what the group thought.

**KEY POINT:** Stay true to who you are as a business. If there are core things that are fundamentally a part of your business, don't lose them during a tough time. Instead, lean into them and refocus the team accordingly. And it's never a bad time to do good.

# Day Hacking

If there's one thing I've learned about myself during this work-from-home quarantine, it's that my ability to focus is something that very much relies on routine. Going into the office would reset my brain to *Productivity mode.* Coming home would change the setting to what I can only describe as *Relax Yourself, Bro mode.*

The problem is, every day, all day, I'm working from home—and my brain is telling me to take it easy.

## Dividing the Day

Over the last month of working from home, I have found that in the mornings, I have less trouble falling into the trap of being unproductive. Maybe it's because of the coffee, or because most of the house is sleeping, or because I've always been a morning person (okay, it's definitely because of the coffee). Regardless, there's no denying that I'm able to crush it in the mornings.

Looking at how I should be spending my time, about half of what I do is a solo effort, meaning it only requires *me* to get it done. Things like working on client proposals and email responses would fit into that category. The other half of what I do are things that require others: checking in with team members, having our weekly leadership team meetings and Huddles, talking to clients or other leaders, etc.

Given that I'm more productive in the mornings (which means I have more motivation and I'm less distracted), I've started moving things that require *just me* to the beginning of my day. Tasks like calls and check-ins work better in the afternoon. With this approach, I'm optimizing my responsibilities to the times of day when I happen to be able to perform them better.

In other words, things that require my brain, and my brain alone, should be done in the mornings. Jobs that require me and others should happen in the afternoons.

---

**KEY POINT:** When working from home, figure out when and how you're most productive. It might mean scheduling work to be done at various times, or changing up the length of meetings, or rearranging your work setting. The key is to optimize your time so that you're as productive as you can be.

---

## Color-Coding the Calendar

I've always relied on my calendar as the ultimate to-do list. I've learned that if it's not on my calendar, I'm likely to forget all about it. It's why my schedule is the first thing I look at when I start my day and the last thing I look at when I finish.

After a few days of working from home, it became clear that I needed a way to gauge where and how I was spending my time. Was I spending enough time checking in with my team? Or too much time checking in with clients? I was finding it hard to see where I was spending my time. Then I had an idea.

What if I associate a color with various activities and then color-code those activities on my calendar? This way, I could look at a week and see, at a glance, where I was spending my time.

I started by breaking my time into the following categories:

Team activities would be blue. This would include leadership team meetings, one-on-ones with team members, etc.

Client activities would be green.

'Doing Good' activities would be pink.

Health activities would be orange. I debated whether or not to have this one, but as Charles had told me previously, "what gets measured gets done." Therefore, if I wanted to make exercise a priority, I needed to measure it.

I then systematically went through every calendar item for the last month and changed each item to the corresponding color. After doing this, I realized that I was missing a bucket.

Random activities would be yellow. These were things that I didn't want to do, but had (for some reason) agreed to do. I didn't realize how many of these things were on my calendar! I was apparently still working on knowing how to say 'no' to some things.

I then went forward in my calendar for two weeks doing the same exercise. It became crystal clear that there weren't enough blue team activities scheduled. I immediately went to work, correcting that because it was a priority to spend more time with my team during this pandemic, not less.

---

**KEY POINT:** Managing your time as a leader is critical. Give yourself the ability to have an overview of how you're spending your time so you can, at a glance, tell if you're focusing on the right things. And learn to say 'no' to initiatives that are distracting you, especially during times of crisis.

---

# Seek Advice from Mentors

I was eager for my call with Charles. As usual, he was right on time. Behind him on the video screen, I could see his backyard.

"Hey there, Will!" he said, waving a wrench in his hand.

"Hey, Charles! What do you have there?"

He pointed his wrench at a bike, propped upside down in the yard. "Oh, well, I'm finishing a little work on my bike while we talk." He chuckled, "You know I think better when my hands are active."

Personally, I thought better pacing around. That was proving difficult by video, but I committed to trying to do more virtual 'walk and talk' sessions when I could.

"Of course. No worries," I said.

After checking on each other's health, I gave him a brief overview of how our business was doing and the moves we had made.

"Sounds like you're doing the right things," he said as he applied some kind of spray to the chain on his bike.

"It does feel that way. But at this point, I don't know what I don't know. I feel like there are things I'm missing, but I just can't see what they are. I was hoping you could help me see around some corners."

He laughed. "Well, I can certainly try. The first thing I would suggest is to be thinking creatively about cash flow. I know we already talked about some of this. You mentioned you talked to your landlord and your bank. Have you thought about seeing which clients would pre-pay or take shorter payment terms? Or which vendors are extending their payment terms? Either way, if you only get a few wins here and there, it will be worth it."

I wasn't seeing how the suggestion was realistic. "How do I get a client to change their payment terms in our favor, especially at this point?" I asked.

"That'll depend on what you're willing to give them in return. Maybe you give a discount on the price of the project. You'll have to find a win-win with them, for sure, but I bet you can figure something out. Assuming they still want to get the work done, the discounted price might be worth the more aggressive payment terms. And you'll have to decide what that ratio is for you. Maybe you can take a ten percent reduction in rate to get paid two weeks faster."

It just might work. "Great, we'll get on that," I said.

---

**KEY POINT:** During a crisis, always remember that cash flow is the lifeblood of your organization. Look for creative ways to extend your cash flow, such as discounts for early payments from clients and extending payment terms with vendors.

---

"Also, I would be very focused on over-communicating with the team during this crisis. Embrace the mindset that you can't talk to them enough. They want to hear your voice and your leadership team's voice, and they have more questions than you'll think to answer."

"That makes sense," I said. We could be doing a better job with that. It was hard to reproduce the in-person relationships, but we needed to try to do more video calls.

He continued, "And vary how you communicate. I learned this a while back. The more ways you hit someone with a message, the more it sinks into their brain. If you tell someone verbally three times that your company's purpose is to…"

He looked up at the screen and pointed the screwdriver he was now holding at me.

"...inspire happiness..."

He grinned. "If you tell them three times verbally that your company's purpose is to inspire happiness, it will be far less effective than if you tell them verbally once, show it to them in a deck once, and they see it in an email once. Still three times, but because they are receiving it in different forms of communication, it will sink deeper into their psyche."

Of course. That was an essential marketing best practice. How had I not considered it for our team?

---

**KEY POINT: Repeat your message to the team in various formats to get an idea across. Change up the way you communicate and keep up a fairly consistent cadence, especially during times of stress and crisis.**

---

"Last thing. Will, you have an exceptional company and the potential to come out of this crisis stronger. But that will only happen if you're paying attention and communicating well."

I was nodding, but not really sure how to make this rosy picture happen. "How do you mean?"

"Well, think about it. You're probably doing a lot of things differently because you have to, right?"

"Yes, like more video conferencing."

"Exactly. You know the old saying, 'necessity is the mother of invention.' You're doing things differently. Maybe you'll learn that you should have been doing more video chats than phone calls all along. Perhaps that practice will let people work from home more because it cuts their commute and increases their billable time, and maybe they're happier too!"

"I see. Instead of thinking of everything we're changing as something we're doing because we're forced to, maybe we look more deeply and see that the changes are things that will make our business better for the long-term as well."

---

**KEY POINT: Necessity is indeed the mother of invention. You're going to change the way you run your business or your team during a crisis. Look at those changes to see if any of them will make your business better in the long-term. Companies that do this will find themselves coming out of the crisis in a better position than when it began.**

---

"Bingo. Okay, pal, I gotta go," he said, flipping his bike to the upright position.

"Thanks as always for the advice. Have a safe ride!"

As we hung up, I recognized how much I value having a mentor. Having someone like Charles on my side gave me confidence and reminded me I wasn't the only one making big decisions that impacted others.

---

**KEY POINT: Find a mentor or mentors that you can ask for advice. Those relationships are meaningful in normal times and critical in times of crisis.**

---

# Focus

From time to time, I find it better to deliver a message via email. In almost every case, I am a firm believer that important messages should come in person, face-to-face (or, if you find yourself working from home due to a pandemic, then by video chat). But this morning, I wanted to share some thoughts with the leadership team about how best to think about using time. It's always a good lesson, but it occurred to me that as schedules have gotten flipped all around, it might be a good reminder.

*Hello, LT!*

*I wanted to share something with you all this morning in the hopes that it helps you think through how you're spending your time these days.*

*I believe that the most precious commodity that we have is our time. We all get the same amount of it, and how we spend that time will tie directly to the things we accomplish.*

*As leaders, we all have non-variable time in our schedules— predictable scheduled time that we plan and control. The time is put to necessary tasks that must happen, regardless of how many other things are coming your way. It's consistent and always going to be a part of your time as a leader.*

*Then there's our flexible or variable time, which lets us react to and help solve problems.*

***Non-variable focus areas***

*#1—Where is the company headed?*

*Whether you oversee a company, a team, or another person, a leader is responsible for clearly and consistently setting the* company vision. While your goal is for everyone to be aware of and embody this objective, it's your job to set the course.

*#2—Are you on track or does the business need to be course-corrected?*

*Once the Vision/Purpose/Culture has been set, which ours has through our PVTV, it's your job as the leader to continually check in on them and help people to re-center when needed. Remember, you are steering the ship. When it goes off course (and it always will), it is your job to reorient and get everyone back on track.*

*#3—Is the team motivated?*

*Your job is to help motivate the team. Always.*

**Variable focus areas**

*#1—Where are you most needed right now?*

*At any given time, a leader must be flexible (and their schedule must allow for this versatility) to react and help the company or the team through its current challenges. Too many leaders are so rigid with their time that they cannot effectively shift their priorities when needed. Cut down on those non-essential meetings.*

*#2—What do you do best?*

*Each of us has a few superpowers, and great leaders figure out what their superpowers are and spend as much time as they can using them to help the company. It's as necessary to know what you're not great at and to delegate that work so you can spend time where you thrive. Delegation is key.*

*#3—Are you available to solve problems?*

*There should always be open gaps in your calendar. A fully booked leader is too busy to support the team with needs as they arise. Make sure you're keeping time for the "Hey, I need some advice," kind of interactions. Your team, especially now, needs the ability to grab you from time to time.*

*Please reach out if there is anything I can do to help you. (I've left some time open on my calendar.) And remember to look to each other for answers and support as well!*

*Best,*

*Will*

---

**KEY POINT:** Think about your time as a leader. Are you spending it in the right areas? Are you available for your team when they need you? This will be different for everyone, but recognizing how you spend your time is critical to how well you lead.

---

# Taking the First Big Hit

The first big hit came two months and four days into the quarantine. Steve sent me a text that read, '*Call me when you can.*' I knew something had gone wrong. As the head of client relationships, he often would share the quick good news in a text. But texting to ask for a call was a sign that something was bad.

I called right away. "Steve, what's up?"

"I just got off the phone with Mark. RedBrick is pulling back."

"How much?"

"A lot. They want to pause half of the work we're doing with them, immediately. The last two months have been really tough for them and I think they're having to tighten their belts in every facet of their business," he said. "I did everything I could think to do, but this is happening."

We had worked with RedBrick from our earliest days as a young agency. As we'd scaled, they'd given us more and more chances to work with them. At this point, they were our largest client. This cut was going to hurt.

"Mark said that he knew we had a thirty-day clause in our contract that restricted them from making any sudden changes, but he asked if we would consider waving it. They need to start the change immediately."

"What did you tell him?"

"I told him yes, of course. I reminded him that just like always, we want to be the best partner we can be for them."

I had complete faith in Steve's decisions on client relationships. By always making sure we treated our partners the way we wanted

**75**

to be treated, we'd earned industry-leading client retention rates. Now was not the time to change that.

---

**KEY POINT:** Build trust with your team, particularly with your leadership team. Their ability to make calls in the moment, knowing you have their back, is critical during times of high stress. As a leader, trust-building should be a priority, and a constant effort should be put toward it.

---

"That was the right call. Is the next step to prioritize the work going forward?"

"Yep. Already started that process."

"You're the best. I'll call Rachel. I think this will force us into Scenario Two, but I'll double-check with her to see if there's any wiggle room."

"Sorry, Will. I know this wasn't the news you were hoping to get today."

"True, but we knew there was a possibility of something like this. We're as prepared as we can be for it, and you did all the right things," I said.

As soon as we hung up, I dialed Rachel.

"Hey, what's wrong?" she asked.

"What makes you think something is wrong?" I asked.

"You only ever call me out of the blue if something is wrong," she said. Apparently, just like Steve, I had a tell.

"Yes, it's bad. RedBrick is pausing fifty percent of their work starting immediately. I'm pulling up the financial dashboard now. Let's make the adjustments so we can see what the impact is."

As I logged into the dashboard, I could see that she was already in it. She adjusted the revenue, and sure enough, it dropped us in the range to pull the trigger on Scenario Two. It meant twenty-percent salary cuts across the board.

"Okay, Will. We're looking at salary reductions." She reiterated what we both were seeing.

"I was really hoping we wouldn't have to do this," I said. "I assume we need to implement the cuts right away?"

"We do. But this is why we told everyone salary cuts were a possibility; so that they could prepare."

It was true. We had been very clear about this from the beginning. We'd done what we could to help the team be as ready as possible. Rachel and Martha had talked to each person over the last month, offering guidance where needed about ways to budget, knowing this risk existed.

"Okay, I'll craft a note to the leadership team and set up a call with them for later this afternoon. And since tomorrow is Huddle, I suppose we will tell everyone on the team then," I said.

"Sounds like a plan."

We hung up, and I sat for a moment to think about what this meant. While it was true that we hadn't had to resort to layoffs like many other companies, this brought us one step closer to that step. If we couldn't hold steady from this point on, we'd lose team members. And that was something I was going to try my hardest to make sure didn't happen.

# Delivering Bad News

Everyone was on the video chat, and a leadership team member had just finished delivering the PVTV.

"Before we get into the numbers, I wanted to share some unfortunate news," I said. I had decided it would be best to just jump right into it. "We found out yesterday that RedBrick is reducing the amount of work we're doing with them by half. Of course, that means we'll also earn half of the amount we were expecting with them."

It was weird to deliver this news over video conference, but the format allowed me to see people's faces clearly. Some were stoic. Others were unable to hide their shock and dismay. A couple of people turned off their cameras. I made a mental note to follow up with them to make sure they were okay.

"Because of the impact that this change will have on our numbers, we will have to implement the second scenario we told you was a possibility. Right now, that means we are not doing layoffs but everyone will take a twenty percent pay cut. It's effective immediately."

I let the news sink in for a minute, then continued. "Obviously, this was not something we wanted to have to do. We're going to answer as many of your questions as we can now. After finishing the Huddle, if you would like to speak with me or anyone else on the leadership team, please reach out. We want to help everyone through this the best way we can."

I then opened it up for questions. The leadership team had prepared for what we thought people would ask, and it's a good thing we had. We got the tough one right out of the gate.

"When our numbers come back, will we be paid more salary until we catch back up from the salary we missed?"

"I'll take this one," Rachel said, answering before I could. "We talked about this at length on the leadership team. We will not be paying people more down the road to make up for what we cut during this period.

"We have to remember that with this revenue loss, our expenses are higher than the money we are bringing in. We have to right-size our business accordingly. We're doing everything we can to avoid laying off team members, so that means pay cuts. As soon as we can bring everyone back to full pay, we will."

I was impressed that Rachel would take that hit, and her answer was spot on.

Someone else on the team asked, "But you said earlier that we have cash reserves in the bank as well as a line of credit. Shouldn't we use all of that before we make any pay cuts or other changes?"

"That's a great question," I said. "We are definitely weighing when and how to use the cash reserves that we have when making these decisions. Keeping a certain amount of cash in the bank is necessary. It is the only way we maintain the ability to do things like pay severance if we should need to or to make payroll if a client needs to delay payment to us. And make no mistake, we are tapping into our cash reserve at the moment. We just have to be cautious as to how much we take out."

There were several more questions, such as what numbers we'd need to hit to bring salaries back, and we were prepared to answer them. As always, we led with honesty, and I've always felt that was the best way to communicate with the team, letting the chips fall where they may.

"We are doing all we can, guys. And will continue to do that," Rachel concluded. "As Will said, please reach out if you want advice or have specific concerns about your situation. We appreciate you all so much."

---

**KEY POINT:** When delivering hard news, push for straight, honest communication. Your team can handle more than you think, and they're smart enough to realize what's happening even if you try to hide it. Have the confidence to treat your team the way you'd want to be treated.

---

The meeting agenda shifted to Ahmet, who presented some promising opportunities in the business pipeline. Everyone was understandably a little quiet. I knew they needed time, and having this conversation virtually made it even tougher.

And, if I'm being honest, I was mostly hoping that we would be able to hang on and not enact Scenario Three. We didn't want to have to lay people off. We were making huge efforts to avoid that step, but so much was out of our control. Time would tell.

# Community Service Day

The conversation with the leadership team a couple of days before had been tense as we worked hard to decide if we should keep the 'Do Good' hackathon on schedule. The timing had proven especially tricky, given that it had only been a week since we delayed half of the RedBrick work and cut salaries by twenty percent.

"I think we should cancel the hackathon," Ahmet said. "Everyone is bummed and stressed because of the pay cut. How can we possibly ask them to donate their time to something that isn't going to help us secure more work?"

"I agree," Steve chimed in. "My team members are pretty upset. I'm not sure this is the right time."

Martha cleared her throat to speak. As she appeared on the screen, I could see she looked tired. And for a good reason. Because of her role and her personality, she had taken on everyone's questions and concerns for a week.

What she said next turned the entire conversation around.

"Actually, I think this is exactly what we all need. When we tell them the hackathon is still on, they might gripe a little. But we need something that will pull everyone together and remind them why they love this place and why they love what they do. Using their skills to help others is just what the doctor ordered."

"Are you sure?" asked Rachel.

"Well, as sure as I can be. And lord knows we have the time on our hands since we're doing less work for RedBrick right now," she said.

Ahmet said, "Some people do, yes, but I could use that extra time to work on a few new business proposals. Anything we can do to help win new business right now would help."

"I think we're all missing the biggest reason we need to run the hackathon," said Martha. "These nonprofits are counting on us to help them! We made a commitment to them and they need support now, more than ever. We can't abandon them because the going got tough. That's not who we are. When this is all over, we want to feel good about the way we behaved. Let's keep sight of who we are. The company I remember wouldn't think twice about going through with this event."

If there was a mic in her hand, I'm pretty sure she would have dropped it.

As heads nodded around the video chat, I finally spoke up. "Guys, everything you said was on point and true. But Martha's right. We need to do this for the nonprofits, our community, and our people. And we need to do it with grace by using it as a way to connect with and check in on our team."

We spent the next half hour talking about how to manage this the right way. By the end of the call, everyone was on board, and we had a plan.

---

**KEY POINT: Strive to find ways to bring your values to life even in painful or inconvenient times. Living your values is even more vital during times of high stress, and it offers a positive way to stay connected to team members you're seeing less.**

---

The day had arrived for our 24-hour hackathon to help a few nonprofits in our community. This was the idea that the leadership team had gravitated toward because it was part of our 'Do Good' initiative. It would inspire happiness, both for the people we would serve and for the people in our company. The work would be fulfilling, exciting, and accomplish a lot of good in a little time.

Individually we wouldn't be working 24 hours straight, but our company as a whole would be. We created eight-hour shifts, breaking the team into three areas: *Strategy & Planning, Design & Flow*, and *Development & Testing*. Each group would have eight hours to get their part of the work done, then hand it off to the next team. By the end of the 24 hours, five nonprofits would have the website or digital marketing support they needed to be stronger and more capable of meeting their goals.

The original plan was for me to roam throughout the process, helping where I could. With the process shifting to a virtual one, I decided to spend time working with each group. We also decided to have coffee and snacks delivered to the home of each person when their shift started. Even though it was an added expense, Rachel agreed right away that we should do it.

The next 24 hours were a blur. There were some bumps here and there—but the work got done and got done well. The nonprofits were grateful, and the teams were proud of themselves and one another.

From start to finish, this group of people was positive, collaborative, and committed to the work and each other. I was reminded of just how special this team was. It was amazing to see everyone sharing and living out the company values.

Years ago, when our company was just starting to take shape, we decided to make sure we hired against our values first, experience second. We looked for a special set of personal characteristics. The decision was paying off now in big ways. Even though the going had gotten tough and people were hurting and nervous, they still stepped up. They supported one another and others whose needs were even greater than our own. And they did it with the grace we expected.

This group was the most cohesive I had ever worked with or led. I couldn't have been more proud of them.

---

**KEY POINT: Hiring for values and culture is always the right thing to do. But especially during a crisis, when true colors will start to show, it will help immeasurably to have people who believe the same things and who work well together. Having well-articulated and acted upon values is critical during times of stress.**

---

As the final minutes of the 24-hour hackathon ticked down, I wrote this email to the entire company:

*Dear team,*

*I am awed by your effort and passion over the last 24 hours. You have made the difference for five nonprofits that are working to make the world a better place. The staggering amount of work you did will make a huge impact on our community.*

*Most of all, I'm humbled to be your teammate. You never hesitate to rise to the occasion. I love you all. Get some rest. You've earned it.*

*Best,*

*Will*

Pushing send, I smiled at how fortunate I was to work with so many amazing people. And then I fell into the most restful sleep I'd had in weeks.

---

**KEY POINT:** Sharing with your team how much you appreciate and care about them is always a good idea. We need more heart in business. Bring the heart.

---

# Relieving Stress

"I'm not overreacting, Ahmet. Honestly, I'm surprised you'd even suggest that!" Martha said.

We were only ten minutes into the leadership team meeting, and things were tense. The team had been on edge for the last few sessions. Little by little, they were arguing about a growing list of seemingly mundane things.

"Whether or not people are getting enough exercise while on quarantine isn't something we should be worried about. It doesn't even seem like something we can or should try to affect," Ahmet replied.

"I guess we have a different opinion on the importance of the mental health of our team members, then," she said.

I normally try to let the team hash out their debates without intervening. Usually, someone speaks up, the team members share their individual opinions, we debate, and the decision gets made. Once it does, we agree to get on board and move forward as a team.

But this was going beyond the typical debate.

"Alright, let me jump in here for a minute," I said. "We have a lot to do on this call, and one of them is to make sure everyone is okay. Martha, how about you work with someone on your team and come up with some ideas for checking in on everyone's general well-being and for sharing healthy lifestyle tips?"

"Will do," she said, a bit out of sorts but satisfied and ready to move on.

The rest of the meeting progressed in a similar pattern. Someone would bring up a topic. Another person would argue strongly for the opposite side, and debate would ensue. The exchanges were feeling more competitive than productive. By the time the meeting ended, we were all exhausted. I needed to figure out what was going on.

Coincidentally, I had a call scheduled with my friend Dale, who was a terrific people leader. I admired him and how he shaped group interactions. Maybe I'd bounce this one off of him.

"Dale! How the heck are you?" I said as soon as his face popped up on the video screen.

"Oh, you know, just living in a world I don't recognize anymore, having to change everything I do," he said with a laugh.

"I know the feeling. How's business?" I asked.

He told me his business had been hit hard. They had to lay people off pretty early in the pandemic. I could tell he was still feeling the effects of that decision, but he was an experienced and graceful leader who was looking forward to better times for everyone.

"How about you, Will? How are things in your world?" he asked.

"An hour ago, I would have said things were about as good as they can be. We have had one big client scale back, which forced us to enact a twenty percent salary cut across the board. But the leadership team was prepared for it, and with so many companies laying people off, I think our team understands that we're relatively lucky."

"So what happened within the last hour?" he asked.

"We had a leadership team meeting. It wasn't pretty. Normally, the group is really agreeable. They're great at kind and courageous debates. But lately, our discussions have become antagonistic," I said. "It's throwing me off. Does this make sense?"

"Well, of course, it does," he laughed. "Think about it...we're several months into what is likely the most difficult time of their careers. From what you've told me about them and the company, I'm guessing they feel very connected to your business. And that probably means they are putting an immense amount of pressure on themselves right now. The pressure has to come out somehow, doesn't it?"

"Huh. I guess that makes sense. They carry the weight of the business on their backs, and they care so much about their teams. Besides having to take the pay cuts like everyone else, they all also feel responsible for the people in their departments. The stress is pretty massive."

"You know, this is something I've been thinking about," Dale said. "All the time, but especially during the hard times, part of the role of a leader is to amplify good and dampen stress."

I pulled out my notepad and began to write as he continued with his thought.

"Leaders can amplify the good by celebrating wins and encouraging people when they accomplish something. This is so important, but it can be tough. I have struggled with it because I'm a growth-oriented entrepreneur. I'm always moving forward. Always. Sometimes I don't take the little time it takes to give an atta-boy that would help someone feel good about the hard work they're doing."

He shook his head humbly at the idea of his shortcoming, and said, "I try to keep this in mind. Instead of reacting to good news with something along the lines of, 'That's done? Great, now look at this next thing we need to tackle. Let's go!' I take the time to recognize it."

"I can relate to that," I said. "I'm constantly looking ahead to the next mountain we'll need to climb so I can make sure my team is ready. As the captain of the ship, I have to navigate us to safe waters and point out where land is."

"Right, it can be hard to remember to celebrate the wins," he said.

---

**KEY POINT: Always remember to share the excitement you feel for your team members when they are successful. When you are proud of them, make sure they know. This is especially important during a crisis. Your team members need to know they're appreciated and loved.**

---

"That all makes so much sense," I said. "But what about the other side of your philosophy? Especially right now, it seems like I need to figure out how to dampen stress more than anything. Have any good tips on how to do that?"

"Maybe it would help to look for opportunities during this crisis to emphasize the good when it happens. Help them to see the big picture and understand that you'll get back on track together."

"And check in with them often. I suggest a weekly video conference with each team member. Don't just jump straight into

**89**

business objectives during leadership meetings. Start by talking about how they're feeling and be honest about how you're feeling. It's okay for them to see that you're struggling too. Actually, it's important."

"That's great advice," I said. "I really appreciate it, and I'll start right away."

"There are a few other things you should consider if you haven't already," he said. "Giving people a sense that there is a plan in place helps put people at ease. Even if the plan is flexible, it's good for people to know there is a plan."

"That's one we've done, but I can be sure to keep emphasizing where we are in that plan and how it has evolved."

"Perfect. And continue to be as open as you can about where things sit. I know you do that already, and I'm sure you're trying your best to be even more open and transparent right now."

"We are, but I bet we could continue to improve," I said.

We chatted for a few more minutes and then agreed to create a more frequent cadence of check-ins during this time.

As soon as I hung up, I began scheduling check-in calls with my leadership team. It seemed like such a simple move—just to talk with people I genuinely liked. I couldn't believe I'd missed it, but I wasn't going to waste any time.

---

**KEY POINT: As a leader, one of your goals is to help relieve the stress of your team, especially your leadership team. Find ways that work for you to do this, and remember to be authentic and vulnerable.**

---

# Learning to Pivot

"Will!"

Shera always spoke with an exclamation mark. It was one of the many reasons she was one of my favorite clients.

"Hey, Shera!"

Before I could ask her how things were in her world, she jumped right in—talking quickly.

"You'll never believe what the last few weeks have been like for us! I'm sure maybe you would, you're probably going through changes as well. It's just that we've pivoted again, and we're already off to the races, but of course, you've seen us pivot before and even helped us through it. Actually, we could use your help right now, which is good news for you, I guess! I thought when this crisis started, we might become stagnant, but we're really just hitting our stride..."

She continued for a few more minutes, probably breaking some kind of record for not taking a breath between sentences.

I decided to break in. "Hold on! You're pivoting again? Tell me about it!"

Pivoting is when a business changes its core business, typically to adapt to changes in the market. It was a very common strategy with startups, but very difficult for non-startups to embrace.

She laughed. "Oh, right, yeah! We're pivoting again. We realized that in today's market and probably after this crisis settles down, our customers will need something different than what we're currently providing. We support salespeople! The sales process is changing!"

"But, your business is doing so well with the current offering, right?"

"It is, but that doesn't mean it will be for long. We're already starting to see a shift in signups, and our customer churn rate is increasing. The numbers are still good, but the signs are there. We need to change. And quickly."

Churn rate often refers to the annual percentage rate that customers stop subscribing to your service (or stop being a customer).

She went on to explain the changes they'd be making, and they made sense. But what really impressed me was how comfortable she was making those changes.

"Was this one of those ideas you came up with on your long runs?" Shera was a long-distance runner and once told me she doesn't run with headphones so that she can think. Many of her best ideas had come on runs.

"Nope, we asked everyone to brainstorm. One of our design team members came up with the idea. Everyone loved it, and now we're off to the races!"

I was energized just listening to her. "That's great, Shera!"

"Honestly, any company that isn't taking a hard look at their business to spot where they might need to shift to retain customers now and in the future is missing a big opportunity."

I made a note to talk to my leadership team about where we could make some productive changes.

"That's so smart," I said. "Now let's talk about how we can help you with this pivot!"

"I was hoping you could!" Shera said.

I wasn't expecting to get new business on this call, but Shera was always good for a few surprises.

**KEY POINT:** During a crisis, look at leading indicators of what might be happening to your business. Try to get in front of major changes, and be willing to shift your business to survive. And always be looking to see if those changes are, in fact, necessary for your long-term success. Remember that every member of your team is a source of incredibly valuable perspective.

# The Power of Networking

"I have great news, everyone!" Martha said as soon as we were done with PVTV.

Martha's good news normally revolved around some way to help our team members (given her role over human resources). But this time she surprised all of us.

"Last Friday, I was on a board call for Keep Love Alive. It was weird not doing it in-person, but we still made some good progress," she said.

"So what's the good news? I'm dying to know!" said Ahmet.

"I got not one, but two leads from other people on the board!"

"What? That's incredible!" Rachel said.

"One lead is from a new board member. She mentioned on the call that they were in the process of trying to find a partner to help them with their new website. As soon as I got off the call, I did my best Ahmet impression and called her up. Sure enough, she said she'd be sending me the RFP later today."

Ahmet laughed. "And you'll connect me with her ASAP?"

"Of course! I just didn't want to spoil the surprise," she said.

"That's so great!" I congratulated her, remembering my conversation with Dale. "And the other lead?" I asked, unable to restrain myself.

"Remember last year when we decided to try to get our clients on these boards with us? I was able to get Ashley from PlayAll Sports to join. She emailed me after the call and said she wanted to talk to us about some work she needed. I already emailed back and copied in Kay from your team, Steve. I know this isn't why we're on these boards, but it sure is a nice perk," she said.

A few years back, I had challenged each leadership team member to join two nonprofit boards. There was some pushback, but everyone eventually found nonprofits they were passionate about. And many of them had shared how much they enjoyed it.

This news couldn't have come at a better time. It really energized the leadership team. Networking has always been the best way to grow our business, and when you can combine doing good with doing well, it's a true win-win.

---

**KEY POINT:** Networking is one of the best ways to find new clients and build deeper relationships with existing clients. There are many reasons for your leaders to join nonprofit boards, the least of which is you might find new clients through doing so. Growth is an all-hands-on-deck effort and making it part of everyone's responsibility will pay off in spades. And people want to work with people they trust.

---

# A Devastating Blow

I emailed the leadership team:

> *Hey everyone,*
>
> *I set up a call for 2:00 p.m. today. We just found out that WHC has had to pause all work until further notice. This puts us over the forty percent drop in revenue. We all know what this means. Please be prepared for a very tough conversation.*
>
> *Will*

This was the worst possible news. Even with the new projects we were discussing that Martha had uncovered in her nonprofit board meeting, we still weren't even close to covering the gap that WHC pulling out would cause. And besides, those projects hadn't signed yet, so we couldn't bank on them.

We had worked with WHC for two years. The CEO had become a friend and was devastated to have to make the call. He already had to lay off half his own staff—and he knew that pausing the work with us meant we would probably have to take that same horrible step too.

"I know this news is as difficult for you all as it is for me," I said to the leadership team. "But we knew this was a possibility, and we've made it almost five months without having to do any layoffs," I paused and rubbed my eyes. "I know that doesn't mean much now, I'm just trying to find the silver lining here."

Rachel took over. "Okay, let's just get into it. I've done the math, and unfortunately, we have to cut twenty of our team members. This will be brutal, but doing this quickly will allow us to give them all decent severance packages. Will and I discussed this, and we're going to use our cash reserves to give them as much severance as possible."

"Isn't there anything else we can do?" asked Martha. She was holding it together as she always did, but the tears were visible.

"Unless someone can find a source of significant new revenue, I don't think there's anything else to do. We've been over the numbers *ad nauseum*, and we've exhausted all other options. I think this is it," I said, sadly resigned to the difficult task ahead of us.

We talked about team members, deciding who would need to be laid off. We went back to our original notes, but so much had changed since then that we had to all but start over. As Rachel has predicted, it *was* brutal.

Then we spent time talking about how we would tell the team. Five months in, and we were still working remotely. The video element added a layer of complexity to an already untenable situation.

We decided that we'd schedule a group call with the group of twenty, during which I'd tell them all at the same time. Leadership team members would have one-on-ones with people in their departments immediately after. At the same time when the twenty were being told, we would have Martha talk to the rest of the company on a separate video conference, informing them of what was happening.

Because we had to get the necessary paperwork in order and rehearse what we would say, we decided the earliest we could do it would be the next morning. But we didn't want to send out random calendar invites, so we'd wait until a half-hour before to send them out.

Solemnly, we all signed off from the video conference. We spent the rest of the day working on the plan, and the feeling of pain deep in my stomach only grew as the day went on. While I knew it was required for the long-term survival of the company, I was devastated.

# The Big Moment

Our plan was to send out the invite at 10:00 a.m. for a 10:30 a.m. video call with both groups. We had meticulously gone over what we were going to say, even picking apart the language in the intentionally vague meeting invites.

At 9:50 a.m., I received a text from Shera that said, "How available is your team right now?"

Curious what that meant, I replied back, "We have some availability, what's up?"

"We're done mapping out our pivot strategy, and it turns out we need a pretty massive overhaul of our tech platform. My staff can't do it all. Can you guys help? It would be a rush. The goal is to launch in 45 days."

I read and re-read the text. Could this be real? I looked at the time—9:52 a.m. We were supposed to send out the calendar invite to everyone in eight minutes. Should I postpone? Would this project be enough to hold us up? I wasn't sure how big this work would be, but at a minimum, it would likely cover half of the gap we now had after WHC went on indefinite pause.

Before I could finish my thought, a video conference invite popped up on my laptop. It was from Steve. I quickly answered it.

"Steve, you won't believe the text I just got!" I said.

"Well, before you get to that, I have some incredible news!"

"Okay, you first," I said, sure his news wouldn't be better than mine.

"Remember those two leads that Martha told us about from her Keep Love Alive board meeting? Well, I was able to get them both to commit this morning, and the new one is also signing up for the PR services that the team came up with last week!"

How coincidental. After I had my call with Shera and she had told me that one of her team members came up with their big pivot idea, I had a meeting with the entire company and challenged them to do the same. One of those ideas was to help our clients with Public Relations during this time. It was a service we had never offered before, but we had the team members with the skills to do it. I loved the idea, and Steve immediately went to work getting the offering in front of our clients.

"I was doing some math...," he said, looking down at a sheet of paper. "And I think this helps us with about half of our deficit from WHC. I know it's not the whole amount, but maybe it will help us spare a few people from the layoffs?"

I glanced at my watch. It was 9:59 a.m. Martha was surely about to hit send on the invites. I smiled into the camera and said to Steve, "Actually, I think we just saved everyone. I gotta go!"

I quickly hung up, leaving him in a state of confusion, but I had to stop Martha from sending the invite. I rang her up via video conference, and while it was ringing, I quickly texted her just in case she wasn't in front of her computer.

"Hey Will," she answered with a clear tone of sadness in her voice. "I'm just about to hit send on the invites."

"Don't do it!"

"What?" She was clearly confused. Maybe she thought I'd lost my nerve.

"I don't think we have to do layoffs! I think we just had our prayers answered, at literally the last second!" I said.

The tears I'd seen in Martha's eyes the day before were back. But this time, they were full of happiness and relief.

---

**KEY POINT:** While tough decisions have to be made, never lose the faith that the work you've been doing may pay off at the last minute. Save a little bit of optimism for a miracle to happen. You never know, it just might.

---

# SECTION THREE: SCARRED, BUT SMARTER

# Back to Normal-ish

The pandemic lasted another month. We were indeed able to keep our heads above water with the new work, and we never had to lay off any team members. We had needed to maintain the twenty percent salary reduction, and I wasn't sure how quickly we'd be able to remove that constraint. But we were alive and intact.

It was a big day. Everyone was coming back into the office.

I got to the office very early. The clock on the wall said 5:44 a.m. That sounded right because I had been awake since 4:30 a.m. But it seemed odd because I was in no way tired. I was the most excited I'd ever been to go into the office—six months away will do that to a person.

Making my way to the coffee machine, I thought about how much we'd been through over the last half-year. How much *everyone* had been through. The world would never be the same. Our business would never be the same. Probably, none of us would be the same as individuals.

I caught up with Charles over the weekend, mostly to check in on him, but of course, he gave me exactly the type of wisdom that I needed.

"So tomorrow's the big day, back to work and all," he said.

"Yep, I literally can't wait to get back to the office! The cleaners are doing a deep clean as we speak."

"And I'm sure you have big plans for everyone," he said.

"You know it. Mainly, I want to challenge the team to share what we have learned during this time. I'm eager to see what they come up with."

"That's great. I'm excited for you too…" Charles paused. "I have one piece of advice for you, Will. I expect it won't be easy for you, the way you're wired."

I was curious and nervous to hear what he was thinking.

Charles continued, "I want you to try hard to be patient. Be patient with how quickly you try to get everyone back to normal and with how quickly you add more plans and start reshaping things. One of your greatest qualities is your ability to bounce back and turn a bad situation into a positive one. But right now, you need to be patient. Not everyone will be at the same place when you go back to work. Take your time, and as much as you can, ease back into it."

I was bummed because he'd always been right in his counsel to me, but this wasn't what I wanted to hear. "Oh man, Charles, that's the opposite of what I was thinking and the opposite of how I'm feeling!"

"I know, Will. But think of it like this—your company has been through a trauma. If someone on your team had been in a serious car wreck, you wouldn't be trying to rush them back to work on their first day back, would you? No, of course not, you'd ease them into it, checking in on them to make sure they were okay.

"You have to realize that while you're eager to get going, most people are nervous for many reasons. The stress they have been feeling isn't just going to fall away. Take it slow, my friend, and listen. Observe. Be there for your team. You're in this for the long haul. There's no reason to rush back too quickly."

He was right, of course. I would have to work hard to go slow and be there for the team. I actually set a reminder on my phone every morning at 8:00 a.m. that said, "Bro, go slow. No, slower."

The coffee was ready, so I poured myself a cup and walked over to my desk. I sat down and looked out over the empty office. And I smiled.

---

**KEY POINT:** After any major problem, and especially after a crisis, take your time getting back to normal. There's plenty of time, so focus on how everyone is feeling. Be there for them personally. Listen more, and know that people will progress at their own pace. They, and you, have been through trauma.

---

# Lessons Learned

On Wednesday after Huddle, I gathered everyone in the company together and divided them into three groups, according to our core Tenets: *attract and retain exceptional people, build remarkable products and experiences, and strive for operational excellence.* We had decided long ago that these Tenets were how we were going to achieve our Vision, so it made sense to look into these three areas to see where we could improve.

The teams spent an hour each and then presented their recommendations back to the rest of the company:

Attract and retain exceptional people

➤ More video conferences for a human connection

➤ Check-in on team member's stress levels and help to manage it with offerings like yoga classes and counseling sessions

➤ Look to build up with contractors and freelancers as we grow to give us flexibility if another recession should hit

Build remarkable products and experiences

➤ Continue developing and selling PR services

➤ Quarterly brainstorm on potential new service offerings

➤ More frequent check-ins with clients to be aware of their business and industry

➤ Everyone in the company should network more, because (as we learned) you never know where the next client relationship will come from

Strive for operational excellence

➤ Aggressively save and protect our cash position

➤ Creatively structure payment terms with clients and vendors

➤ Look for ways to be more efficient with our time (possibly shorter meetings, etc.)

➤ Everyone should have a time optimization plan for how they spend their days

➤ Dig into how much office space we need and what work from home options we can offer now that we have shown we can run successfully in a remote situation

Each of their ideas had come from what we learned during the crisis. I was very proud of what they had come up with. But of course, the real work would be to execute these ideas. And I'd be careful not to rush too many of the ideas, per Charles's advice.

---

**KEY POINT:** After a crisis, assess how you performed and diligently look at the new ways you will operate the business. Learning from a crisis (and our mistakes) is the best way to grow as a leader.

---

There was one more thing I wanted to put in place...

# Cash is King

Rachel looked at me and grinned.

"Okay, out with it," she said. "I know you've got some big idea cooking, what is it?"

I smiled. I did have a new idea, though it wasn't *mine*, per se. I'd long been a student of leaders like Warren Buffett, who espoused the idea of amassing cash for any number of strategic reasons.

"I'd like us to put a plan in place, now that we're through this crisis, to save up enough cash to be able to pay our employees for a year with no income coming into the business."

"That sounds really interesting," she said. "But please remember, we're not through this crisis yet. Even though we're back to work, there will still be ramifications going forward."

"Yep, good point, and one that I'll make to the team in our next Huddle," I said. "But back to the idea, what do you think?"

"Well, I'm a finance and operations person, so yes, that sounds fantastic, but give me some reasons why. We'd obviously be restricting our growth a bit by doing that, taking money we'd normally invest in efforts like marketing, sales, and new services so we could save it up for a rainy day," she said.

"Right, that would be the trade-off. My thought is first, if we're building a forever company, which we are, then our survival is first and foremost. The idea that we have to hit fifty percent growth next year instead of ten percent doesn't really matter when you think about the company from that long-term standpoint. A hundred years from now, it won't matter that we had more or less growth, only that we grew...and survived."

Rachel nodded, so I continued, "So that's the first reason. Also, imagine what we could do during a crisis or recession if we had that kind of stability. We could invest in building products that we don't normally have the time for. We could look at acquisitions of other companies to bolster our services and add new talent. We could help more of our nonprofit partners, helping them provide their services to the people that really need it. We could literally come out of the crisis being stronger for it."

"Okay, you don't have to convince me anymore," she said. "You had me at 'save cash.' I'll work up a plan."

This approach would be a big change for our company. We've been wired for growth since day one, and we had big plans for spinning up new service lines and investing in growth. But coming through this crisis helped me to see a new path forward, one that gave us the freedom to think about the long-term health of the company, and I was sure going to take advantage of it.

---

**KEY POINT:** If you are building a forever-business or even a business that you don't expect to sell for at least five years, then consider building up a massive cash reserve. More and more, we are a global society, one where any number of forces happening in any number of places could wildly disrupt your business. The next crisis is likely around the corner, and the more cash you have on hand, the more confident you can be that you'll survive it.

---

# EPILOGUE

Two months had passed since the company had been able to come back to work. The effects on the economy had started to ease, and our numbers were starting to show it.

Charles and I were having lunch at Naan, our favorite restaurant. It still felt a little weird, and the restaurant was not as crowded as it once had been.

I looked around and observed, "I think it's going to take a while for things to get back to normal, if they ever do. I did hear they're doing a ton of take-out business, maybe that's where things will net out for retail."

"Possibly," agreed Charles. "Tell me how things are going for you."

"We reinstated everyone's full salary," I was happy to report.

"That's great to hear," Charles said.

"Yep, that was a good moment," I said.

"And what do we have here?" he asked, looking down at the paper I had brought with me. It was a list of traits that we had outlined that successful entrepreneurs seemed to have. We had been working on a thought experiment with the question being, could a non-entrepreneur embrace these characteristics?

"Looks like we have 14 different traits. That's still far too much. I think we need to get it well below ten," he said.

"I know if this ever becomes something we'll need to simplify it. Just don't force me to fit them into some kind of silly acronym," I said.

He laughed. "Now, how did you know my mind was going there? No, of course not...unless it happens naturally."

Just then, my phone buzzed with a text message. I normally had my phone on silent, but I must have forgotten. I took a quick look down at it. It was a message from my old colleague, Matt. I heard he had gotten a big promotion at the company he'd joined after we worked together at Crackersnap. It'd been a while since I saw him, I wonder what he wanted.

Luckily Charles excused himself to go to the restroom, giving me the chance to read the text. It said:

> *Hey Will, hope you're well. We're about to issue a big RFP for our brand and advertising business. Let me know if you guys want to be included.*

Huh, well, that could be interesting. Maybe we'll throw our hat in the ring.

I just hope Matt hasn't changed too much.

**Has Matt changed? What happens with the RFP? Find out.**

The story continues in *The 5-Day Turnaround*.

# THE
# 5-DAY
# TURNA
# ᗡNUOᖉ

*Be the leader you*
*always wanted to be.*

## JEFF HILIMIRE

# THE 5-DAY
# TURNAROUND PRELUDE

"And that's our pitch. We'd love to know what you think!"

Silence.

To be honest, I had expected a bit of post-pitch silence. Our team at the agency had worked long hours over the past three months to give Matt and his team a significant amount to consider.

After reaching a few dead-ends, we came up with a big idea—an approach with the potential to disrupt an entire industry. It was one of the most promising business solutions we'd ever created at my agency. I couldn't wait to hear Matt's reaction.

Asking a prospect to break new ground is always risky. One thing I've learned is you never know how your audience will react to a truly daring concept. During the pitch, I was aware of Matt's body language and, at times, felt he was getting it. At other moments, he seemed lost in thought.

Was it indecision I was sensing?

When we worked side by side at Crackersnap Tech in the past, Matt and I were a great duo. We were even known to finish each other's sentences on occasion. Right now, that all seemed a long time ago.

"Excellent!" Matt exclaimed, breaking my train of thought. "We asked you to push us, to really challenge us. Speaking for everyone here, I can say you did just that."

The rest of his team, including those who were less attentive earlier, nodded their heads. The one exception was the newest member, a woman named Meredith. From the start of the pitch to the finish, she took notes continuously, which is generally a positive sign.

"Thanks!" I responded to Matt. "Do you have any questions for us? We can walk you through the timeline if you like. Building a new approach to target buyers is something we would do with your technology team—"

Matt cut me off.

"Actually, I think we're good on the details for now. We really appreciate your team spending so much time on this one. As you know, today was the last of the presentations we've scheduled. Now the work begins on our side before we can make a decision. Thanks again for coming."

Matt's polite words were not the enthusiastic response my team had hoped to hear.

He stood up to leave, and we all followed.

As my associates packed the display boards and made small talk, I made my way over to where Matt was standing.

"So, are we still on for coffee tomorrow morning?" I asked.

"You bet. It gives me a chance to bring you up to speed on the process we'll follow the rest of the way. Excellent stuff today, Will. You sure were in top form."

We said our goodbyes, yet I had the feeling he was holding something back. Once in the elevator, our team congratulated one another on a job well done. I could sense their relief that the pitch was behind us. Mostly, I was looking ahead to my first good night's sleep in a while.

Matt and I first met when we both worked at Crackersnap Tech, an artificial intelligence and technology startup. He reported directly to the CMO, and I was in charge of sales. We left soon after Crackersnap was acquired by a big conglomerate ten years ago.

He moved on to become CMO of Titan, a Fortune 1000 company. I went on to become a VP at Ideathon, a highly regarded problem-solving consultancy. After four years spent mostly setting stalled companies on a new path, it felt right to risk being an entrepreneur with my own startup. Now, I'm running a thriving, six-year-old digital ad agency. Things are going well. We've grown to just under 100 employees and have gained some impressive clients. Winning Titan would bring us our largest account so far.

Who would have thought back then that pitching to be Matt's Agency of Record would be part of our future?

Matt and I did a good job of staying in touch after leaving Crackersnap. Luckily, our current business offices are only a ten-minute Lyft ride apart. We keep up with each other by getting together now and then at The Steaming Cup—our favorite local coffee spot.

Matt's move up the corporate ladder was no surprise. I always saw him as a person with impressive talents, including a mix of creative ideas and a down-to-earth knack for getting the job done.

I was eager to hear what Matt thought of our pitch. Drifting off to sleep that night, it was tough deciding which was more likely—a thumbs-up or a thumbs-down.

As usual, I was at The Steaming Cup in the morning well before Matt. It's my habit, when meeting someone, to get there early for some undisturbed email time. Matt, as was his custom, strolled in at 8 a.m., exactly as we had agreed.

"Over here!" I waved to Matt. "The line was getting long, so I grabbed your usual black coffee. Don't worry. I won't put it on your first invoice."

Matt laughed nervously. The obvious reference to the pitch made him uncomfortable. My attempt at humor was something I regretted almost at once.

What struck me as we started sipping our coffee was how much older Matt seemed to be. It was as if the last few years had taken quite a toll.

"So, busy week?" I asked, restarting the conversation.

"Yeah, always. But busy is good, right? I gotta say, though, I've never felt so underwater. Even after adding two team members, it's hard to keep up. Things change so fast these days!

"And the pitch process to land an agency was a pain—no offense to you guys. You did great. It's some of the others we've seen. The repeated briefings. All those requests for more data. The maneuvering to get an edge. The endless presentations to sit through. I never knew there were so many different lines of attack an agency can come up with and still end up in the same place," he complained.

"It's rough on the agencies as well. We work our tails off for weeks, and at best we have a 30% chance of winning. That's the industry average."

Matt looked up from his coffee. "Really? Those seem like tough odds."

"Yep, nature of the beast. If I had known how tough it was to win new clients, I might have chucked the whole agency gambit."

I quickly corrected myself. "No, that's not true. The process of solving problems with new ideas is so exciting. Also, there are lots of great people to work with on both the agency side and the client side."

Matt shook his head. "Huh, sounds like the old Crackersnap days…and the complete opposite of what it's like at Titan."

What came next is what I dreaded hearing.

"Which is why I don't think we can choose your agency to work with us on this project."

"Oh," I said, with a sick feeling at the pit of my stomach. "Well, I sure did appreciate the chance to pitch. Sometimes we nail it, and sometimes we don't. I get that."

"No, Will. Actually, your take on the challenge we're facing is perfect. Seriously, it's the kind of thinking we need to outdo those newcomers eating our lunch. My team admires what you came up with," he reassured me.

Matt stood up and walked over to the counter for a coffee refill. I stayed at the table, coming to terms with what he just said.

"Gotta say, I just don't get it," I started right off when he rejoined me. "With all those positives, why didn't you choose us? Is it the price? We can look at the scope. I know we were a little over your budget, but we can work on that."

"Nope, your budget was fine, no worries there. Several other estimates were higher than yours. Honestly, the reason we can't work with you is—and I really hate to admit this—we could never pull it off. It's not doable for a team with our limitations."

I pressed for a better answer. "Meaning what exactly?"

"Look, the reality is we're like every other established business. We spend most of our time in meetings. When we try to implement anything to break the mold, we over-complicate and over-process it. During the years I've been here, the number of times we went 'all out' in a genuinely new direction comes down to zero. I've learned to settle for marginal gains we can make work."

He had trouble meeting my eyes. I guessed he was embarrassed by what he was saying.

"But at Crackersnap you were the champion of reaching for the stars despite the risks!" I exclaimed.

"Titan isn't Crackersnap, Will. And we're not unique. I have friends at other large companies that have been around forever, and they struggle with the same constraints. Put simply, they don't know how to move with the speed of a startup. That's why up-and-coming entrepreneurs are kicking our butts. You should know, some of the winners are your clients!"

He was right. My agency works with both established brands and hot new startups. As you'd expect, the startups move much faster than the big guys. In fact, sometimes they go so fast we have a hard time keeping up with them.

Rather than respond to Matt, I decided to get my own coffee refill. What I needed was a few minutes to think through a wild idea that had just crossed my mind.

Maybe losing the pitch was not a done deal.

What if I could help Matt turn around his situation to become more like the startup where he once thrived? If that happened, he'd be able to work with our agency after all. What was racing through my head was all those CMOs I put on the right track when working at Ideathon.

Coming back to the table, I fired a question at Matt. "Did you mean it when you said your team loved our approach, but you lack confidence in them pulling it off?"

Matt came back with, "On one hand, your proposal outclasses anything else we've seen. On the other hand, with the culture at Titan, we could never make it happen."

"Matt, please excuse my being blunt, but walking away from a marvelous opportunity is not the you I remember."

I continued, gaining strength. "Do you recall how we had to overcome stumbling blocks at Crackersnap each time the company's growth stalled?"

"Sure do. Sorting out the real problem worked every time. Once we identified the actual hurdle, a solution began to take shape," he agreed.

"Matt, you're facing a similar challenge now. Backing away from taking bold action at Titan keeps your team from doing their best. The answer is to bring about a sea change that allows you to be the leader you truly are."

Suddenly curious, Matt asked, "What are you getting at?"

"Why not hold off on making your agency selection for another month or so," I proposed. "During that time, maybe we can get together one day a week to figure out how your team at Titan can act more like a successful startup. Overall, it would take just five days of your time." I paused. "Are you with me so far?"

"Will, is there something in your coffee? This sounds a bit…"

"Crazy?" I said, finishing his sentence, just like in the early days of our partnership. "Trust me. Everything I saw about turning thinking around while running Ideathon meetings tells me we can pull this off. All I'm asking for is one month's delay in choosing an agency. That still leaves time for you to go with any shop you want if what we proposed yesterday still doesn't seem actionable. All your options remain open."

I waited a few seconds and then pushed to close the deal. "What do you say?"

Matt looked at me, squinting his eyes a bit, deep in thought. He took a long drink of coffee, set the cup down, and asked, "Do you honestly think it's possible to change Titan in our five days together?"

My answer brought a smile to his face. "You bet I do! Remember, we are not trying to change all of Titan just yet. This step is about evolving how your team gets things done. We turned around more formidable situations at Crackersnap in less face-to-face time. To change your team's behavior, you've got to make the first move. With your revamped leadership, they can do a u-turn in far less time than you think."

"I have to admit I'm intrigued," Matt said. "And there is room in the schedule for a delay in making my agency choice." He was doing the math in his head, his fingers tapping as he made the calculations.

Matt looked straight at me and said, "Will, I need to weigh the pros and cons. What I can agree to for now is an answer, one way or the other, in a phone call tomorrow evening. Is that okay with you?"

"Absolutely," I said. "Just call my cell."

"Perfect," Matt responded.

We shook hands and spoke our goodbyes. Matt headed for the parking lot, and I fired up the Lyft app to request a ride.

Tomorrow, I would know the answer. If Matt went for The Five-Day Turnaround, my agency would still have a chance to win the account. What had just happened at The Steaming Cup left my heart pounding.

A glance at my Apple Watch showed there was still time to get to my first meeting of the day.

While riding to my client, SalesLive, I was sorting out next steps should we get the go-ahead in tomorrow's phone call. The toughest part would be staying in sync with Titan norms while bringing about a flip-flop in the culture of Matt's team.

Thinking about what we would encounter, I recalled a comment my mentor Charles had made recently. "You know when companies first start out, they're trying to do what has never seen the light of day before. If success follows, all the energy and passion they put into making the early days a triumph shifts to protecting what they built. Soon the company's growth slows down, and further progress is minimal. It's the trap every established company faces."

Something I hadn't shared with Matt was that Charles and I have been collaborating on an article for Harvard Business Review about the many ways the mindset at startups and grown-up businesses differ. Charles is a generation older and a brilliant entrepreneur. Our joint research has identified the top traits of successful startups. Lately, we've been exploring how those traits might be adapted to unlock growth at companies that have left their startup culture far behind.

My mind was buzzing with how my talks with Charles could be used to support Matt's about-face.

I turned into the parking lot and focus quickly shifted to my meeting with Shera, the CEO of SalesLive. She personified the very traits I admire in successful startups. Maybe Shera being my first contact after the morning chat with Matt would prove to be a good omen.

**Keep reading!**

*Get your copy of The 5-Day Turnaround on Amazon.*

# APPENDIX

## SECTION 1: BEGIN THE BEGIN

### Find the Right Words

As a leader, whenever you are talking with your team, prepare. This is especially important during a crisis. Words are important.

### The Preparation

At every major decision point, go back to your company's or team's purpose. Having a credible, honest purpose is the key to building a great team, and it is required to survive in a real crisis.

Tell your team how you're going to start strong, what you envision the end will look like, and that the middle is up to them. Paint an optimistic picture and remind them of their strong foundation. They need something or someone to give them guidance and confidence, and something to act on.

### The Mindset

Short-term decisions will need to be made during a crisis to stay alive as a business. Always weigh those against the long-term ramifications and never forget who you are. Integrity is key.

As a leader, especially during a crisis, you need to make sure you're focused on the operational aspects of the business and the emotional state of the team. Stay close to your leadership. They are on the front lines. They're your primary source of insight about the state of the culture. And they'll need you more than ever.

A positive, optimistic leader is magnetic. People want to follow them. This may not be a natural state for you, and it will likely be more difficult during times of high stress, but keep in mind that your team is watching you for signs of how to behave. You can do this.

## Working from Home

When working from home, be purposeful about productivity. Find ways that work for you, even if it requires 'tricking' yourself into it.

## Financial Planning

Create a financial and operational plan going into a crisis. Even if you alter it as you go, it is crucial to take the time to consider all the details when you aren't in the throes of a recession—or any disaster, for that matter. Having a plan will give you peace of mind and allow you to make better decisions in the future.

Make sure you have diversity in your client base. That means controlling the percentage of revenue a client comprises, varied deal structures, and a spread across multiple industries. This diversity will help when trouble hits, crisis or otherwise.

Focus on growth. Too often, teams will work hard on new business, get some wins, move their attention to other things, only to look up six months later and realize their sales pipeline has dried up. A consistent growth mindset—more than strategy, case studies, or any other sales concept—is the vital area of focus.

Save *at least* two months of expenses in cash. Try to establish a line of credit with your bank equal to that amount. You don't have to use it, but you never know when disaster will strike. As your company grows, always look to increase your cash on hand and your line of credit accordingly.

Do everything you can to preserve cash. Pull from your line of credit, ask your landlord if you can defer rent payments, talk to your vendors, and see if you can get extended payment terms—anything to give yourself more runway to make it through a recession.

Be willing to think creatively about the things you can do to help keep your company alive. Ideas such as cutting everyone's salary might seem untenable at first, but it might be the best decision if the alternative is laying off team members. Only you will know the right course to take, but make sure you're thinking creatively and evaluating all possible options.

# SECTION 2: GET OUT THE MAP

## Open-Book Management

Consider an open-book management style. It can feel uncomfortable sharing your finances with your team, but it will pay off in spades with increased trust and better problem-solving. Communication builds trust, and trust is what makes any team work.

During a crisis, knowledge is everything. Stay close to your customers and partners, and share liberally with your leadership team (and overall team when appropriate). The name of the game is agility. The more you know, the better you can react.

## Windmills vs. Walls

Understand when something needs to be changed only for the moment vs. when it can be a change that can help your business overall. Look at big changes, especially during a crisis, as a way to grow and get better. We always learn the most when faced with a challenge.

## Weekly Huddle

During difficult times, rely on those closest to you for support and ideas. You're not alone, and ideas can come from anywhere. Seek input from anyone who will give it to you.

Your team needs to know you have a plan. For the long-term, for the short-term, and certainly during a crisis. Sometimes *having* a plan is more important than the plan itself.

Always go back to your PVTV: Purpose, Vision, Tenets, and Values (or your specific construct). If you have worked to bring your PVTV to life within your company, it can be the compass that everyone uses to navigate through difficult times.

Find ways for your team members to acknowledge and recognize each other publicly. During a stressful time, this kind of peer support and recognition will go a long way to strengthen bonds.

## Bank Relationship

Work to maintain a personal relationship with the account manager at your bank. If that's not possible at your current bank, get a reference and make a change. There will be hard times in your business, and having a personal connection with your banker will be extremely helpful.

## Keep Learning

During a crisis, it's even more important to be growing and learning. Try hard not to stop processes you have in place for this, and perhaps look for new ways to add learning into your time.

## Doing Good

Stay true to who you are as a business. If there are core things that are fundamentally a part of your business, don't lose them during a tough time. Instead, lean into them and refocus the team accordingly. And it's never a bad time to do good.

## Day Hacking

When working from home, figure out when and how you're most productive. It might mean scheduling work to be done at various times, or changing up the length of meetings, or rearranging your work setting. The key is to optimize your time so that you're as productive as you can be.

Managing your time as a leader is critical. Give yourself the ability to have an overview of how you're spending your time so you can, at a glance, tell if you're focusing on the right things. And learn to say 'no' to initiatives that are distracting you, especially during times of crisis.

## Seek Advice from Mentors

During a crisis, always remember that cash flow is the lifeblood of your organization. Look for creative ways to extend your cash flow, such as discounts for early payments from clients and extending payment terms with vendors.

Repeat your message to the team in various formats to get an idea across. Change up the way you communicate and keep up a fairly consistent cadence, especially during times of stress and crisis.

Necessity is indeed the mother of invention. You're going to change the way you run your business or your team during a crisis. Look at those changes to see if any of them will make your business better in the long-term. Companies that do this will find themselves coming out of the crisis in a better position than when it began.

Find a mentor or mentors that you can ask for advice. Those relationships are meaningful in normal times and critical in times of crisis.

## Focus

Think about your time as a leader. Are you spending it in the right areas? Are you available for your team when they need you? This will be different for everyone, but recognizing how you spend your time is critical to how well you lead.

## Taking the First Big Hit

Build trust with your team, particularly with your leadership team. Their ability to make calls in the moment, knowing you have their back, is critical during times of high stress. As a leader, trust-building should be a priority, and a constant effort should be put toward it.

## Delivering Bad News

When delivering hard news, push for straight, honest communication. Your team can handle more than you think, and they're smart enough to realize what's happening even if you try to hide it. Have the confidence to treat your team the way you'd want to be treated.

## Community Service Day

Strive to find ways to bring your values to life even in painful or inconvenient times. Living your values is even more vital during times of high stress, and it offers a positive way to stay connected to team members you're seeing less.

Hiring for values and culture is always the right thing to do. But especially during a crisis, when true colors will start to show, it will help immeasurably to have people who believe the same things and who work well together. Having well-articulated and acted upon values is critical during times of stress.

Sharing with your team how much you appreciate and care about them is always a good idea. We need more heart in business. Bring the heart.

## Relieving Stress

Always remember to share the excitement you feel for your team members when they are successful. When you are proud of them, make sure they know. This is especially important during a crisis. Your team members need to know they're appreciated and loved.

As a leader, one of your goals is to help relieve the stress of your team, especially your leadership team. Find ways that work for you to do this, and remember to be authentic and vulnerable.

## Learning to Pivot

During a crisis, look at leading indicators of what might be happening to your business. Try to get in front of major changes, and be willing to shift your business to survive. And always be looking to see if those changes aren't, in fact, necessary for your long-term success as well. Remember that every member of your team is a source of incredibly valuable perspective.

## The Power of Networking

Networking is one of the best ways to find new clients and build deeper relationships with existing clients. There are many reasons for your leaders to join nonprofit boards, the least of which is you might find new clients through doing so. Growth is an all-hands-on-deck effort and making it part of everyone's responsibility will pay off in spades. And people want to work with people they trust.

## The Big Moment

While tough decisions have to be made, never lose the faith that the work you've been doing may pay off at the last minute. Save a little bit of optimism for a miracle to happen. You never know, it just might.

# SECTION 3: SCARRED, BUT SMARTER

## Back to Normal-ish

After any major problem, and especially after a crisis, take your time getting back to normal. There's plenty of time, so focus on how everyone is feeling. Be there for them personally. Listen more, and know that people will progress at their own pace. They, and you, have been through trauma.

## Lessons Learned

After a crisis, assess how you performed and diligently look at the new ways you will operate the business. Learning from a crisis (and our mistakes) is the best way to grow as a leader.

## Cash is King

If you are building a forever-business or even a business that you don't expect to sell for at least five years, then consider building up a massive cash reserve. More and more, we are a global society, one where any number of forces happening in any number of places could wildly disrupt your business. The next crisis is likely around the corner, and the more cash you have on hand, the more confident you can be that you can be that you'll survive it.

# ACKNOWLEDGMENTS

I t would seem that every significant effort takes a team. Anything meaningful I've accomplished in life has been through the help, support, and partnership of others.

This book, as you might expect, was no exception.

And given that I wrote this book *during* the COVID-19 crisis of 2020, everyone who helped did so as the world was falling down around them.

To all of my dragons at Dragon Army—I've never worked with a more passionate, more talented, and more 'Team First-y' group of people. Your incredible competence and dedication gave me the freedom to spend the necessary time to write this book, and for that, I thank you so, so much.

To my various editors and team members who helped make sure this book was put together well: Michael Stanley, Andrea Whitcomb, Katie Foster, Cortney Rosen, Erica Warhaftig, Jenn Leahy, Ashton Lane, and Dorothy Miller-Farleo (DMF!). And Jennifer Jessen, my beautiful sister, who read and edited the book while quarantined and recovering from COVID-19!

To the ultimate editor, Rachelle Kuramoto, who I am so blessed to work with every day. Your tireless, can-do spirit and obvious writing talent inspire me more than you know. Thanks for keeping me honest while I tried my best to put words on the screen in an order that makes sense, with you graciously and patiently re-ordering them, so the sentences and overall story was, well, you know...coherent.

To Jessica Carruth, my book partner-in-crime, who was the first person I told that I wanted to write and publish this book—in a little more than 30 days. (Our first book took about a year, start to finish). Not only did you not quit on the spot, but you also did what you always do. First, you asked, "Are you sure?" and then quickly got to, "We can do this!" Thank you for saying yes and for working so hard to get this book across the finish line. It wouldn't have happened without you.

To Jenn Leahy and Ashton Lane, for so, so much. Immediately after the COVID-19 pandemic hit us in mid-March, my dear friend Ryan lost his battle with cancer. I was devastated (and still am). For several weeks after that, you two grabbed hold of our company and steered the ship, allowing me time to grieve. Ashton, as I'm sure you can tell, a great deal of this book is a reflection of your financial expertise and wisdom. And Jenn...I've never, in my 20 years of leading businesses, had to hand the reigns over to another person. I did so during this period to you with no hesitations, and you surpassed even my lofty expectations. You are a treasure.

To my kids, Zac, Drew, Kaitlyn, Hannah, and Kai, who never cease to inspire me and brighten my days. It was a joy writing this book while the five of you spiraled around our house, us being all locked in there together during the quarantine period. In fact, given that I wrote *The 5-Day Turnaround* in the same manner (then we were locked up together in Scotland on holiday), perhaps that's the only way I know how to write books.

And to my wife, Emily, who always supports me, and who I can't imagine going through this crazy thing called life without.

# ABOUT THE AUTHOR

J eff Hilimire is a best-selling author and an accomplished entrepreneur who has launched multiple organizations, and who has successfully sold two companies. His current business, Dragon Army, is one of the fastest growing digital experience agencies in the nation. Over the course of 20 years, Jeff has helped guide leaders from some of the most well-known global brands to mobilize growth using a startup mentality. He also co-founded 48in48, a global nonprofit that produces hackathon events, building 48 nonprofit websites in 48 hours.

When Jeff isn't running Dragon Army, mentoring, or volunteering at 48in48, he is working hard as the founder of Ripples of Hope, a collection of for-profit and nonprofit organizations focused on business as a force for good in the world.

Jeff lives in Atlanta with his lovely wife, Emily, and their five children. You can follow Jeff's adventures on his personal blog, jeffhilimire.com.

Made in the USA
Middletown, DE
20 October 2020

22429880R00080